The Loafer's Guide
To
Successful Retirement
And
Slow Cooking

Victor Friedmann

With

Michael Petrale

Published in the United States of America by Lulu.com

ISBN 978-1-4303-2579-6

www.lulu.com

Book design by Victor Friedmann

To

Lynn and Hans,
Dearest Friends.
For All The Love and Good Times Our Families Shared.

Vic and TJ

AKNOWLEDGMENTS

*Bull Market is a random market movement causing an
investor to mistake himself for a financial genius.*

I began this project while convalescing from a serious leg fracture. This work prevented me from bemoaning my miserable condition and it also forced me to formulate and analyze the course of financial retirement planning. Far from working in a vacuum, this project gave me the opportunity to interface with friends, relatives, financial planners, and insurance companies. Many individuals contributed to this project and they helped me recover faster while enriching the value of this book. They all deserve recognition and thanks.

My wife, Toni Jo, nursed me and enforced a strict physical therapy regimen that restored my physical and emotional strengths. She also meticulously edited the manuscript and provided valuable support with the mechanics of word processing software. She loves it when I get technical. Michael Petrale transported me home following surgery at an out-of-state hospital and provided moral support. It is Michael who originally spawned the ideas for this book, who provided me with statistical information on equity-indexed annuities, and who provided critiques and companionship. Lynn Tieman professionally edited the manuscript and injected ideas of her own. Lynn has the enviable talent to verbalize ideas clearly with her unique sense of humor. Lynn's touches dance throughout the book. Cousin Bernard Newman edited the manuscript, reviewed financial concepts, and offered valuable insights of his own. He generously shared his financial knowledge with me. Brother-in-law Ben, a distinguished economist, patiently reviewed the manuscript, offering suggestions and ideas. The humor is for Ben and the recipes are for my sister, Anna, who sought independent opinion on the longevity annuity. Peter Lingane of Financial Security by Design refined my comparisons between TIPS and STRIPS. The Hartford, The Equitable, and MET Life Insurance companies provided quotations for longevity and variable annuities. Over the years cooks from Oman, Italy, Louisiana, Texas, and North Carolina have shared their slow cooking secrets with me.

Victor Friedmann
Durham, NC
2007

TABLE OF CONTENTS

INTRODUCTION

Bear Market is a 6 to 18 month period when the kids get no allowance, the wife gets no jewelry and the husband gets no sex .

Financing retirement and slow cooking take time and neither allows much room for error. Only the prudent investor who is keenly aware of his limited investment savvy and who follows the principle of the magic eight will achieve a financially secure golden retirement. Time, a minimum return on investment of eight percent, and an eight percent savings rate are necessary conditions to finance a retirement budget equal to 80% of gross income.

Currently popular investment instruments known as Equity-indexed Annuities (EIA), as well as fixed annuities, variable annuities, and all types of bonds – Treasury, Corporate, Municipal, and Treasury Inflation Protected Securities ("TIPS") guarantee protection of interest and warrant investment consideration for retirement. Unfortunately, some of these investment instruments are highly illiquid, do not compensate for inflation, and do not pay dividends each year for reinvestment. The returns of many of these investments generally have become eroded to the point that they are unsuitable for the prudent investor.

As a solution, this book proposes an investment in an S&P500 index fund over an optimum ten-year time period. Here is why: The S&P500 pays a dividend, has beaten inflation over the long term, and rarely shows a loss over any given ten year period. More importantly, over long periods of time the S&P500 index has provided total returns that are more than double the return of the investments discussed above. To a loafer's delight, investing in an S&P500 index fund works best if just left alone to work its magic.

This book promotes investing in a total market index, investing early, investing regularly, and staying the course. The book cautions readers that Social Security benefits are likely to decrease in the future and that only the prudent investor able to save at least 8% of gross income and earn at least 8% return on investment will be able to finance a golden retirement. The time and money a loafer saves by avoiding money-losing schemes can be used instead to drink a few cold ones while smoking salmon fillets.

HOW TO USE THIS BOOK

The stock market is weird. Every time one sells, another
one buys, and they both think they are smart.

This is probably the most expensive book you will ever buy because you need only a few numbers to determine your retirement financial plan. The rest of the book focuses on convincing you to leave well enough alone.

Although this book reviews a variety of investment vehicles, it is also a retirement planning handbook. This is a tool that will allow anyone to plan a retirement budget that is realistic and accurate. While the ideal reader is young, has just started in the workforce, and has many years left to accumulate wealth, this book can help even those who are well into their productive years determine exactly where they are headed financially and what changes may be necessary to meet their financial goals. The true value of this handbook lies in the Tables section where complex mathematical relationships have been simplified and condensed into just four parameters. No need to know about ratios or percentages. Just plug and play.

Those readers too lazy to read the whole book or who are familiar with inflation, inflation protected securities, equity-indexed annuities, exchange traded funds, and who have an established history of return on investment can skip immediately to chapter 15, *Your Retirement Budget Planner*, and begin their retirement budget strategy. Readers challenged by the task of balancing a cold beer, paper, pencil, and a calculator are invited to visit the free, interactive, web-based *Loafer* spreadsheet where just a few keystrokes will yield the personalized saving rate required for a golden retirement and estimate the probability of financial failure.

Readers who want to appreciate the developmental reasoning behind the recommendations should read the book from cover to cover. A good understanding of the various investment vehicles along with their associated advantages and disadvantages is fundamental to effective budget planning. If this book motivates just one reader to plan and act for the future, the mission will be fulfilled.

CHAPTER 1: TIME AND MONEY

The best time to buy anything is last year.

Uncle Jacob, who was a successful businessman, believed that time is money and he loved asking trick questions. His favorite went like this:

Suppose you were offered two 15-year contracts. The first contract deposits $1,000,000 in the bank earning 10% per year compound interest. The second contract deposits one penny in the bank, earns no interest, and will double the balance every six months. The money in the account is yours at the end of the 15-year contract.

Which contract would you choose? Think about it and then turn the page.

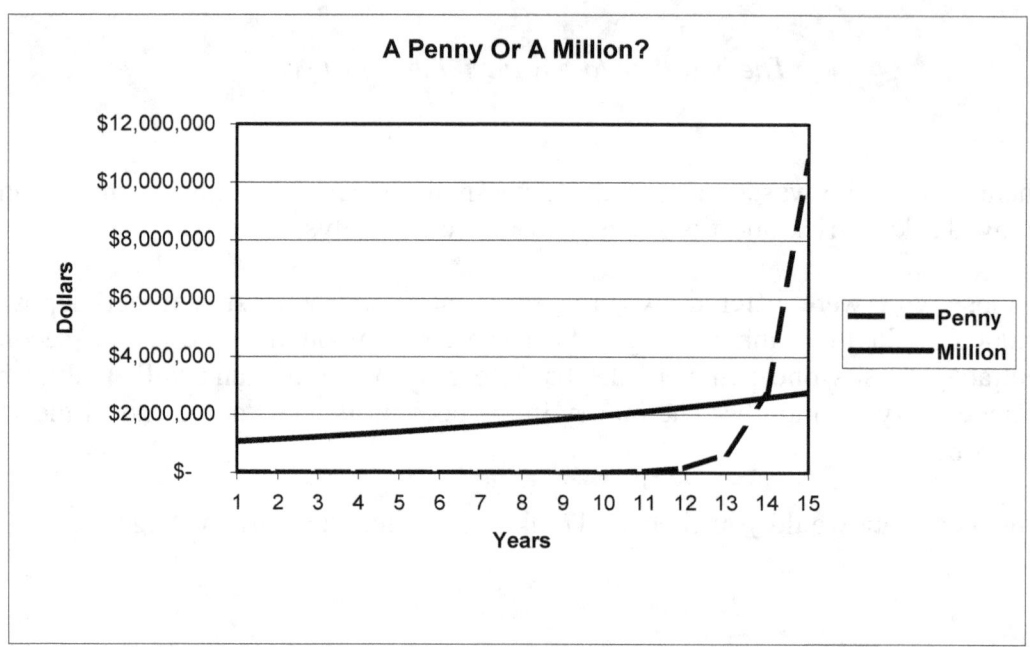

Figure 1
A Penny Or A Million?

Surprised? You shouldn't be. Indeed, time is money and the power of doubling the account every six months overtakes the million-dollar account in 14 years.

Unfortunately, most investment vehicles do not quadruple their values every year; but there are two interest crediting methods worth knowing about—simple interest and compound interest. The difference between these two explains the income limitations associated with inflation-protected securities, issued by the U.S. Treasury.

To appreciate the difference between simple and compound interest consider the two accounts below each starting with $1000, each earning 7% per year—one earns simple interest while the other earns interest compounded every year.

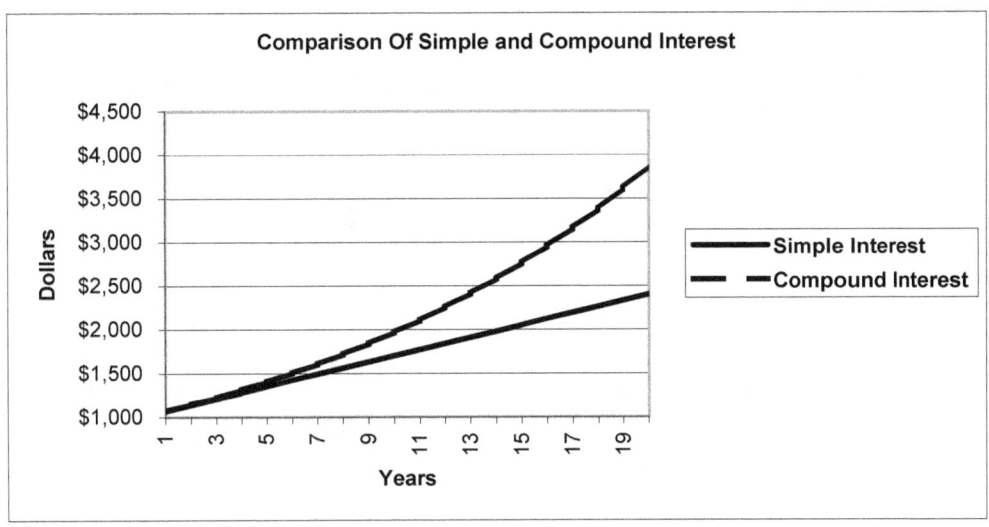

Figure 2
Simple And Compound Interest

The powerful effect of compounding, which means earning interest on interest, is evident right from the start. This fact leads to one of the fundamental rules of successful investing:

Always re-invest investment earnings.

One rule of thumb useful when comparing various investments is the Rule of 72:

> Divide 72 by the compound return on investment; the result gives the number of years required for the investment to double. Alternatively, divide 72 by the number of years required for it to double and the answer is the compound return on investment.

Earning 7% per year compound interest, for example, the $1,000 doubles in just over 10 years. The investment industry uses several terms for compound interest; among these are: average interest, yield to maturity, and internal rate of return. This book uses the term equivalent compound interest, ECI, to include all these terms. The term, equivalent compound return, ECR is interchangeable with ECI.

CHAPTER 2: INFLATION

Economists have forecasted eleven out of the last three recessions.

An understanding of the devastating effect of inflation is fundamental to retirement planning. Inflation is insidious; it is always there, reducing the purchasing power of the consumer. This means that even those investors who manage to keep their capital intact over time still lose because of the loss in purchasing power.

Inflation is defined as the change in the Consumer Price Index, or CPI, a sophisticated economic model that consists of thousands of consumer goods. The economic arm of the U.S. government constantly updates this model to reflect current products and consumer preferences. Consider the history of the CPI over the last 57 years:

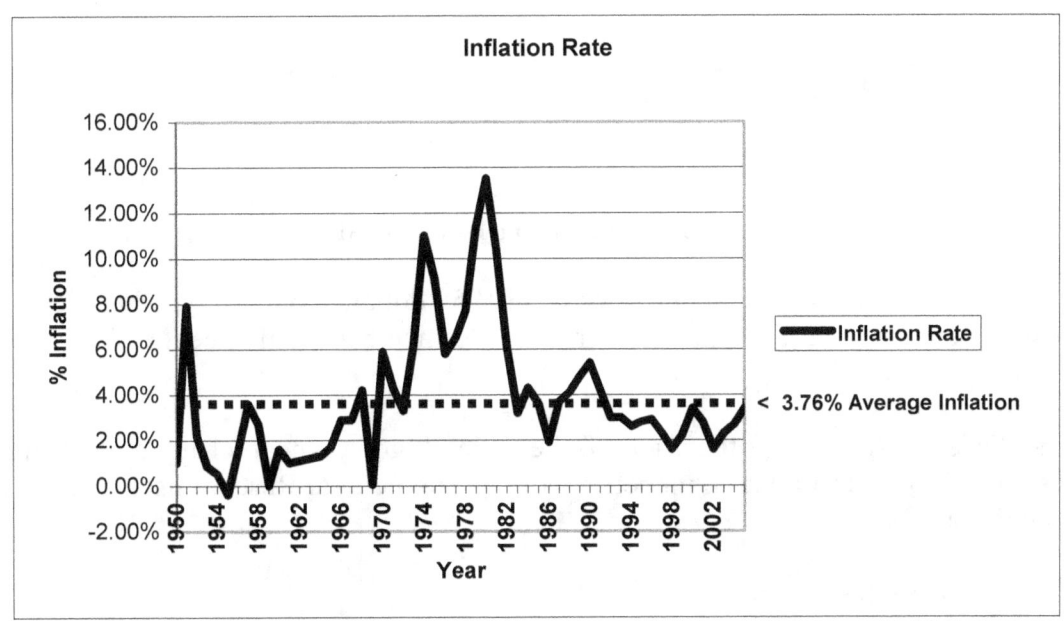

Figure 3
Historical Inflation Rate

From 1973 to 1983 inflation raged, reaching 14%. During those years when investors could earn almost 20% from fixed income instruments such as CDs, bonds, and money market funds the stock market languished. Inflation was not only bad for the stock market; it also hurt the consumer by eroding the buying power of the dollar. Consider the historical impact of inflation on purchasing power.

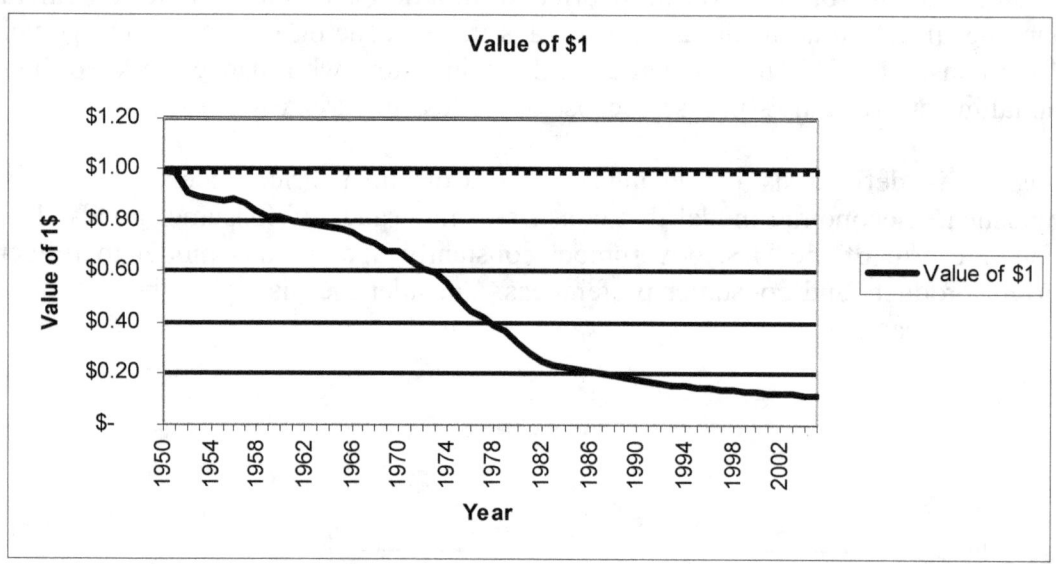

Figure 4
Historical Purchasing Power Of $1

In 2005 $1 could purchase about 12 cents in 1950 dollars; conversely, what used to cost 12 cents in 1950 costs about $1 in 2005. Remember the five-cent Coke or the nickel ice cream cone?

The Federal Reserve is the arm of the federal government charged with the responsibility of formulating monetary policy. The Federal Reserve itself explains its mission best:

Goals of Monetary Policy

The goals of monetary policy are spelled out in the Federal Reserve Act, which specifies that *the Board of Governors and the Federal Open Market Committee should seek "to promote Effectively the goals of maximum employment, stable prices, and moderate long-term interest rates." Stable prices in the long run are a precondition for maximum sustainable output growth and employment as well as moderate long-term interest rates. When prices are stable and believed likely to remain so, the prices of goods, services, materials, and labor are undistorted by inflation and serve as clearer signals and guides to the efficient allocation of resources and thus contribute to higher standards of living. Moreover, stable prices foster saving and capital formation, because when the risk of erosion of asset values resulting from inflation—and the need to guard against such losses— are minimized, households are encouraged to save more and businesses are encouraged to invest more.*

Consider how the goals of monetary policy have guided the Federal Reserve in its reactions to inflation:

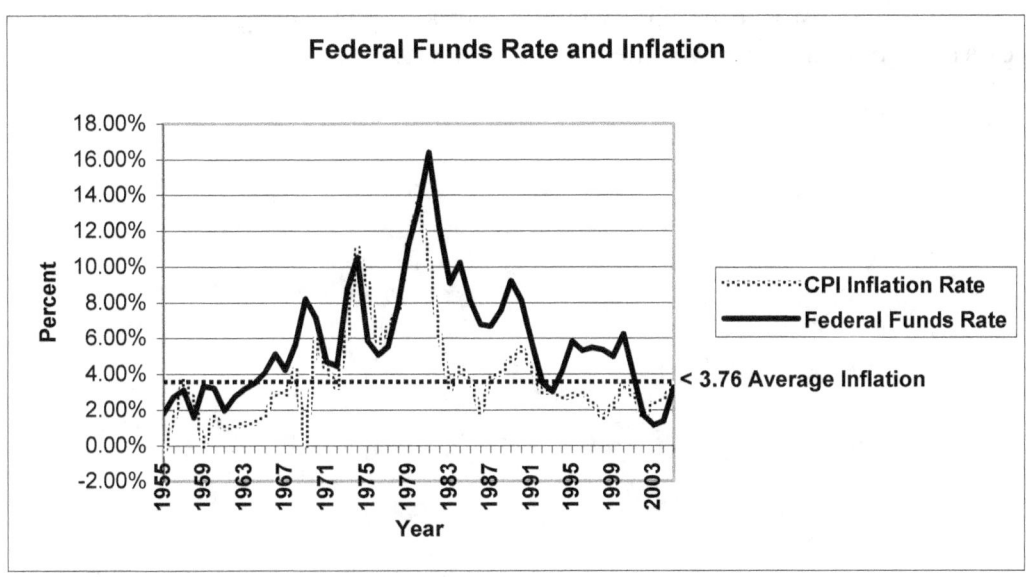

Figure 5
The Federal Funds Rate And Inflation

History shows that one of the primary goals of the Federal Reserve is to stem inflation and one of the tools in its arsenal is the Federal Funds Rate. The Federal Funds Rate is the rate banks pay each other to borrow funds overnight. The "Fed" does not control long term or commercial interest rates. Typically, long term rates change in tandem with changes in the Federal Funds rate but this has not been the case since 2002.

The "Fed" does not publicly state a target inflation rate, but history suggests the Federal Reserve aims for a comfort zone that has inflation running at a rate of about two percent, as measured by the Consumer Price Index (CPI). Furthermore, history suggests a Federal Funds Rate that is two to three percentage points above the current rate of inflation. With fifty years of history, it appears reasonably certain that the Federal Reserve is unlikely to change this aspect of monetary policy. Actions the Federal Reserve may take mirrors its opinion of the near-future course of the American economy.

So, for any given investment, the rate of return must be at least 3.76% just to compensate for the long-term average rate of inflation. Furthermore, investments in taxable accounts must return enough to compensate for both inflation and taxes in order for the investor to remain whole in terms of purchasing power. This book suggests a target return on investment of at least 8%.

CHAPTER 3: CAPITAL AND INFLATION PROTECTED TREASURIES

Market Correction: The day after you buy stocks!

Investment suggests risk; investors who seek to keep their capital intact and also earn a certain percentage above the rate of inflation will find a friend with the U.S. Treasury department. The Treasury offers two securities that return a stated amount above the rate of inflation and also guarantees the principal.

Treasury Inflation Protected Securities, TIPS, and I-bonds, inflation bonds, fill the niche for the investor interested in capital preservation net of inflation. The two securities achieve this goal in slightly different ways and are appropriate under different conditions.

TIPS

TIPS are issued for a minimum face amount of $1000 and have a coupon rate, the nominal interest rate that does not change. The nominal interest rate is designed to yield a real return after inflation of about 2.5%. The face amount is the price of the security when it is first issued. Each bond is pegged to an initial value of the Consumer Price Index, CPI, and has a maturity date up to 30 years from the date of issue. The CPI is adjusted every six months and the change is applied to the face amount. One half the coupon rate is then credited on the adjusted face amount twice a year. This security adjusts the capital for changes due to inflation and the income earned adjusts accordingly also. So, capital and the income earned keep pace with inflation.

TIPS trade on the secondary market, but secondary market pricing is not guaranteed due to fluctuations in interest rates. What is guaranteed is that at the time of maturity accrued interest will be paid, the principal will be adjusted for inflation, and that the principal value at maturation will not be less than the original amount. TIPS, therefore, also protect the investor from disinflation. In other words, only investors who keep their TIPS to maturity benefit from this guarantee. The secondary market refers to the buying and selling of these securities after the original issue. Those who buy and sell on the secondary market may make or lose money. Brokerage houses carry out this trading.

The capital adjustments and interest payments are credited twice a year, but the capital adjustment is paid only when the note matures. This means there is only a small cash flow from coupon payments prior to maturity. Both coupon and capital adjustments, however, are taxed yearly as they accrue. The tax on this "phantom income" suggests that TIPS are appropriate investment vehicles mainly for tax-deferred accounts.

I-bonds

I-bonds, inflation bonds, are issued for a minimum amount of $50 and have a coupon rate, interest rate that does not change. They are issued for 30 years but continue to accrue interest beyond that time if not redeemed. These securities have an inflation adjustment factor that is tied to the CPI, but does not exactly equal actual changes in inflation. This adjustment is usually less than the rate of inflation.

Every six months one half of the yearly adjustment factor is added to one half of the coupon rate; this total interest is then credited to the account. I-bonds can be redeemed at any time. If the bond is redeemed in less than five years a nominal penalty will apply. When redeemed, the investor receives the face amount of the bond and all the accrued interest. There is no income flow prior to redemption.

I-bond phantom income is also taxable in the year it is posted but the investor has the option of deferring tax payments until redemption. This option makes I-bonds a suitable investment for taxable accounts. In the real world most investors defer the tax until the bonds are redeemed.

Have Your Cake And Eat It Too?

When things appear too good to be true, they generally are; so it is with inflation-protected securities. At first, it may appear that the coupon rate, which is the return on investment, is guaranteed over and above inflation for both TIPS and I-bonds. In fact, the actual cash flows between the two securities are different and this difference affects the equivalent compound interest. While TIPS pay interest every six months and pay off the inflated value of the coupon at maturity, I-bonds pay nothing until the bond is cashed in. In other words, I-bonds do not earn compound interest. The equivalent compound interest for I-bonds, therefore, is less than the sum of the coupon rate and inflation.

Consider two investments, one in 10-year TIPS with a 2.5% coupon rate and an I-bond with the same rate held for 10 years. In this model the inflation rate is held at 3% for the life of the securities.

Here is how the TIPS account accumulates over 10 years. Note that each year appears twice to accommodate interest payments every six months:

TIPS COUPON=2.5% INFLATION=3%					
Year	Principal	Earnings	Cash Flow	Coupon Rate	Equivalent Compound Interest
1	$ 1,000	$ 13	$ 13	2.50%	
1	$ 1,015	$ 13	$ 13	2.50%	
2	$ 1,030	$ 13	$ 13	2.50%	5.444%
2	$ 1,046	$ 13	$ 13	2.50%	
3	$ 1,061	$ 13	$ 13	2.50%	
3	$ 1,077	$ 13	$ 13	2.50%	
4	$ 1,093	$ 14	$ 14	2.50%	
4	$ 1,110	$ 14	$ 14	2.50%	
5	$ 1,126	$ 14	$ 14	2.50%	
5	$ 1,143	$ 14	$ 14	2.50%	
6	$ 1,161	$ 15	$ 15	2.50%	
6	$ 1,178	$ 15	$ 15	2.50%	
7	$ 1,196	$ 15	$ 15	2.50%	
7	$ 1,214	$ 15	$ 15	2.50%	
8	$ 1,232	$ 15	$ 15	2.50%	
8	$ 1,250	$ 16	$ 16	2.50%	
9	$ 1,269	$ 16	$ 16	2.50%	
9	$ 1,288	$ 16	$ 16	2.50%	
10	$ 1,307	$ 16	$ 16	2.50%	
10	$ 1,327	$ 17	$ 1,344	2.50%	

Figure 6
Computation Of Compound Interest For TIPS

The yield to maturity, the equivalent compound interest rate, is 5.444% over 10 years; just less than 5.5%, the sum of the coupon and inflation rate. The inflation adjusted return in this example is about 2.444%, just about the advertised rate of 2.5% net of inflation.

The I-bond performs as follows:

Year	Principal	Earnings	Account Value	Cash Flow	Equivalent Compound Interest 4.48%
		I-BONDS COUPON=2.5% INFLATION=3%			
1	1000	27.5	$ 1,028	0	
1	1000	27.5	$ 1,055	0	$ 1,045
2	1000	27.5	$ 1,083	0	
2	1000	27.5	$ 1,110	0	$ 1,092
3	1000	27.5	$ 1,138	0	
3	1000	27.5	$ 1,165	0	$ 1,141
4	1000	27.5	$ 1,193	0	
4	1000	27.5	$ 1,220	0	$ 1,192
5	1000	27.5	$ 1,248	0	
5	1000	27.5	$ 1,275	0	$ 1,245
6	1000	27.5	$ 1,303	0	
6	1000	27.5	$ 1,330	0	$ 1,301
7	1000	27.5	$ 1,358	0	
7	1000	27.5	$ 1,385	0	$ 1,359
8	1000	27.5	$ 1,413	0	
8	1000	27.5	$ 1,440	0	$ 1,420
9	1000	27.5	$ 1,468	0	
9	1000	27.5	$ 1,495	0	$ 1,484
10	1000	27.5	$ 1,523	0	
10	1000	27.5	$ 1,550	1550	$ 1,550

Figure 7
Computation Of Compound Interest For I-bonds

The equivalent compound interest of the I-bond is only 4.48%, substantially lower than its equivalent TIPS. With 3% inflation, the inflation adjusted return for this I-bond example is 1.48%, not the advertised 2.5%. I-bonds are, therefore, not a suitable retirement investment vehicle because their inflation adjusted compound return is low and can actually be negative depending on the life of the bond and the method used in computing the inflation adjustment.

Historically, TIPS yield about 2.5% net of inflation. The total return depends on the current inflation rate. For the last several years the total TIPS yield has been about 5%.

CHAPTER 4: EQUITY-INDEXED ANNUITIES

The safest way to double your money is to fold it and put it in your pocket.

An annuity is a contract between an investor and an insurance company. The investor pays a lump sum or a series of payments in exchange for a lump sum payment or a guaranteed stream of income at a future date. An equity-indexed annuity ties the final value of the annuity and, therefore, the annual payments to the S&P500 index. Equity-indexed annuities offer the opportunity to participate in the stock market with no downside risk because they not only guarantee the principal; they also guarantee no loss from year to year. Sounds too good to be true, and it is; the catch is in the details.

While equity-indexed annuities offer protection of capital, the various crediting methods, participation rates, caps, expenses, and spreads limit the maximum return on investment. The industry offers three major crediting methods, the way the company relates the investor's account to the stock market index. The participation rate refers to how much the investor's account retains from a positive change in the stock market index. An 80% participation rate, for example, means that if the stock market index rises by 10%, the investor's account rises by 8%. Caps refer to the maximum gain that is credited regardless of the performance of the stock market index. With a 9% cap, for example, even if the stock index were to rise by 15%, the investor's account would rise by only 9%. The spread refers to the reduction, or fee, the company imposes on a monthly change in the S&P500. Protection of capital protects both the original principal and the year-to-year changes in the stock index. Negative changes in the stock index result in no change in the investor's account. All these variables affect the net return to the investor.

Year Point-To-Point Crediting Method

This form of crediting the account compares the value of the S&P500 12 months after the purchase of the annuity to its value at the time of purchase. The percent difference is computed. This difference is then applied to the investor's account and reduced to a level called the cap. The cap is the maximum limit allowed for a positive yearly change. The participation rate is simply the percentage of this change that is credited to the investor's account. If the investor, for example, purchased a $10,000 annuity and the S&P500 changed by a negative 5%, the investor's account value remains $10,000. If the S&P500 changed by 15%, a 9% cap with 80% participation means that the investor's account at the end of the first year would be worth $10,720, with the $900 gain multiplied by 80%. The same process repeats year after year until the annuity matures.

A review of several yearly point-to-point crediting methods shows that a liberal plan offers a 9% cap and 100% participation. The caps of 0% and 9% affect the distribution of return on investment for annuities. The distribution shown below is called a bi-modal distribution and for such distributions statistical measurements such as the average, median and standard deviation do not apply.

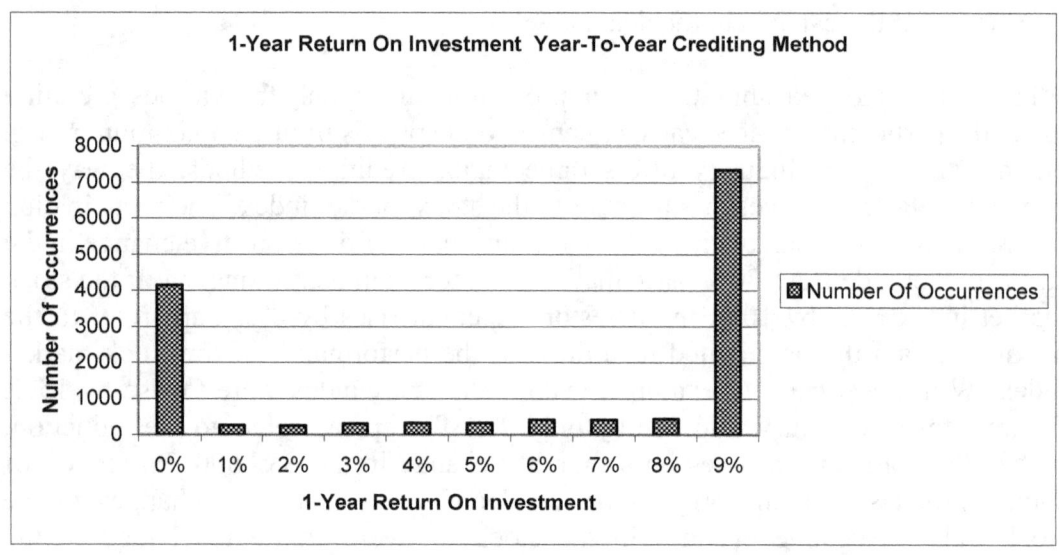

Figure 8
1-Year Return Distribution Year-To-Year Crediting Method

When held for longer periods of time, however, such distributions tend to normalize; they become more like a normal or Gaussian distribution. Statistical measurements of normal distributions are more meaningful. A simulation of the performance of such an equity-indexed annuity held for periods of ten years from 1950 to 2006 yields the following average return on investment:

Equity-Indexed Annuity
Crediting Method
Annual Point-to-point
9% cap; 100% participation
Equivalent Compound Return
5.53%
Median Compound Return
5.54%
Standard Deviation
1.04%

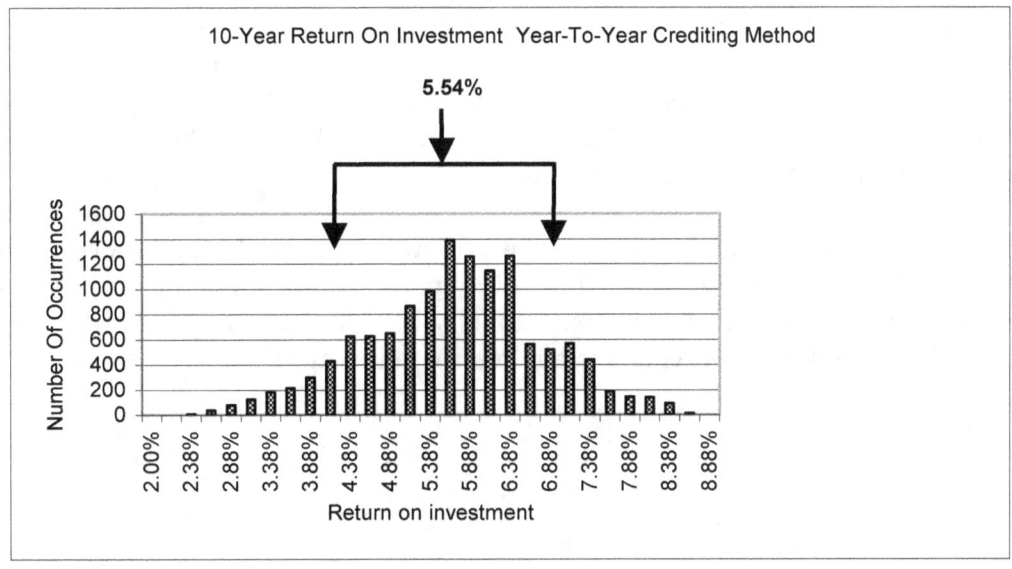

Figure 9
10-Year Return Distribution Year-To-Year Crediting Method

Monthly Point-To-Point Crediting Method

The monthly point-to-point crediting method is similar to the year-to-year method except that it is computed on a monthly basis with a lower cap. Monthly changes are computed for the entire year capped to a maximum by the cap rate. Negative monthly changes remain negative. At the end of the year all the capped monthly changes are summed and the total is then credited to the investor's account. Negative yearly changes are set to zero leaving the investor's account unchanged; the participation rate further reduces the return to the investor. For example, with monthly changes as follows:

-2%, -1%, 0%, 3%, 2%, 1%, 5%, 3%, -1%, 1%, 3%, 1%

After applying the 2% cap factor, for example, the monthly changes would be recomputed as:

-2%, -1%, 0%, 2%, 2%, 1%, 2%, 2%, -1%, 1%, 2%, 1%

The revised monthly changes are summed, multiplied by the participation rate of 80% and the result is credited to the investor's account. A negative change would result in no change to the investor's account. In this example, the sum of revised monthly changes is 9%. This factor is then reduced to 7.2% by the participation factor. If the investor's account had been worth $1,000 at the beginning of the year, it would be worth $1,072 after crediting.

A review of various monthly point-to-point offered by the industry concludes that a liberal offering is a 3% cap with 100% participation. A simulation of the performance of such an equity-indexed annuity held for periods of ten years from 1950 to 2006 yield the following average return on investment:

Equity-Indexed Annuity
Crediting Method
Month–To-Month
3% Cap: 100% Participation
Equivalent Compound Return
5.25%
Median Compound Return
5.57%
Standard Deviation
2.01%

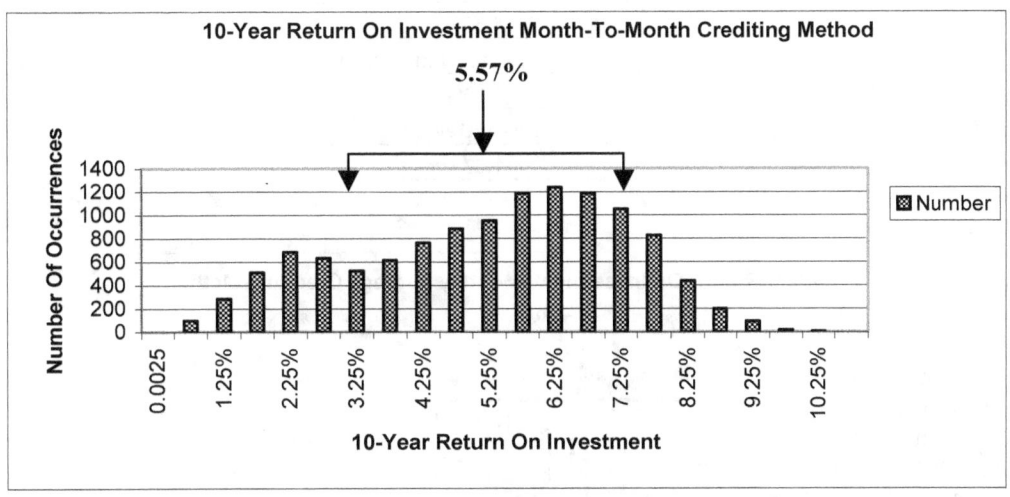

Figure 10
10-Year Return Distribution Month-To-Month Crediting Method

Monthly Average Crediting Method

This crediting method computes the S&P500 monthly average for the current year. This monthly average is compared to the monthly average of the previous year and the percentage change is computed. This change is then reduced by a factor called the spread. For example, if the monthly average value of the S&P500 for the previous year were 1000 and the monthly average for the current year were 1100, this percentage change of 10% would be reduced to 8% with a 2% spread in force.

An investor's account worth $1,000 the previous year would now be worth $1,080. Any negative changes in the average after the spread would leave the account the same.

A review of various monthly average plans offered by the industry concludes that a liberal offering is a 2% spread. A simulation of the performance of such an equity-indexed annuity held for periods of ten years from 1950 to 2006 yields the following average return on investment:

Equity-Indexed Annuity
Crediting Method
Monthly Average
2% Spread
Equivalent Compound Return
4.31%
Median Compound Return
4.26%
Standard Deviation
1.57%

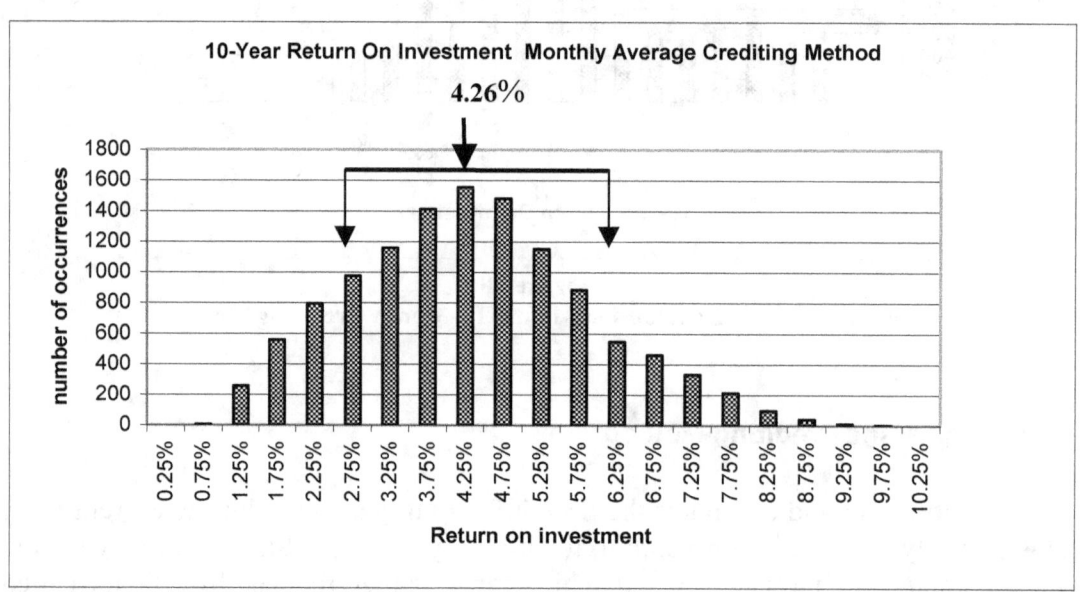

Figure 11
10-Year Return Distribution Monthly Average Crediting Method

CHAPTER 5: THE STANDARD AND POOR 500 INDEX

Economics is an extremely useful method of employment for economists.

What It Is

The Standard and Poor 500 index, S&P500, consists of 500 stocks chosen for market size, liquidity, and industry group representation. It is a market value weighted index, with each stock's weight in the index proportionate to its market value. The S&P 500 is one of the most commonly used benchmarks of the overall stock market. The index was developed with a base level of 10 for the 1941- 43 base period.

Return On Investment

The median 1-year return of the S&P500 without dividends is about 9.56%. This is the conclusion of the analysis of 14,448 daily values organized into 1-year periods from 1950 to 2007. During these years the lowest one-year return was –44% while the highest return was 59%. The distribution of returns within this range is illustrated below:

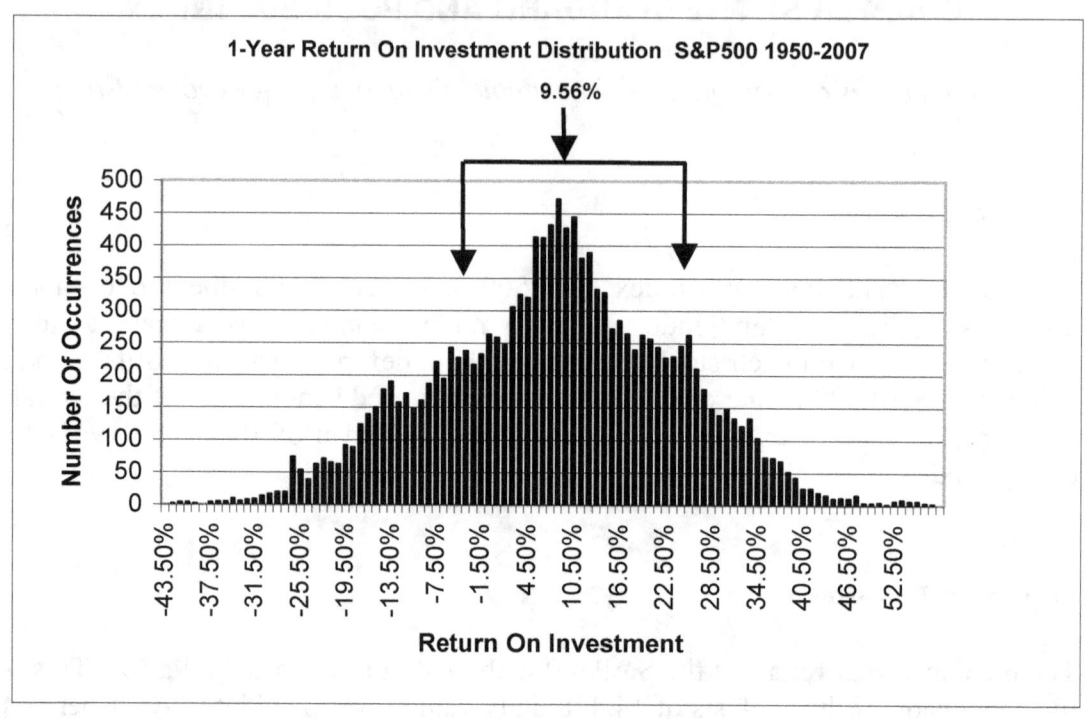

Figure 12
Historical Return Distribution S&P500

The median one-year return for the S&P500 over the last 56 years is about 9.56%, excluding dividends; if reinvested, the average yearly dividend adds about 3% for a total return of 12.56%. This observation is important because equity-indexed annuities do not include dividends in any of their crediting methods. The second important observation is that the distribution of investment returns illustrated in the graph above looks similar to a normal distribution. In a normal distribution 67% of the occurrences will occur within two standard deviations from the median. In the case of the S&P500, the median one-year return is 9.56% and the standard deviation is 15%. This means that two times out of three the S&P500 returns will range from –6% to 24% with the most probable return of 9.56 %.

Successful retirement planning requires the investor to earn at least 4% above the average rate of inflation, or about 8%. Remember that preservation of capital alone does not preserve the purchasing power of the dollar. If the average rate of inflation is 3.76%, prices of goods and services will double in 19 years.

Since the valuation of the stock market can fluctuate widely, it is important to know what the lowest equivalent compound interest, ECI, on investment one can expect as a function of time. In other words, what is the lowest historical return on investment the S&P500 has yielded as a function of years the investment is held?

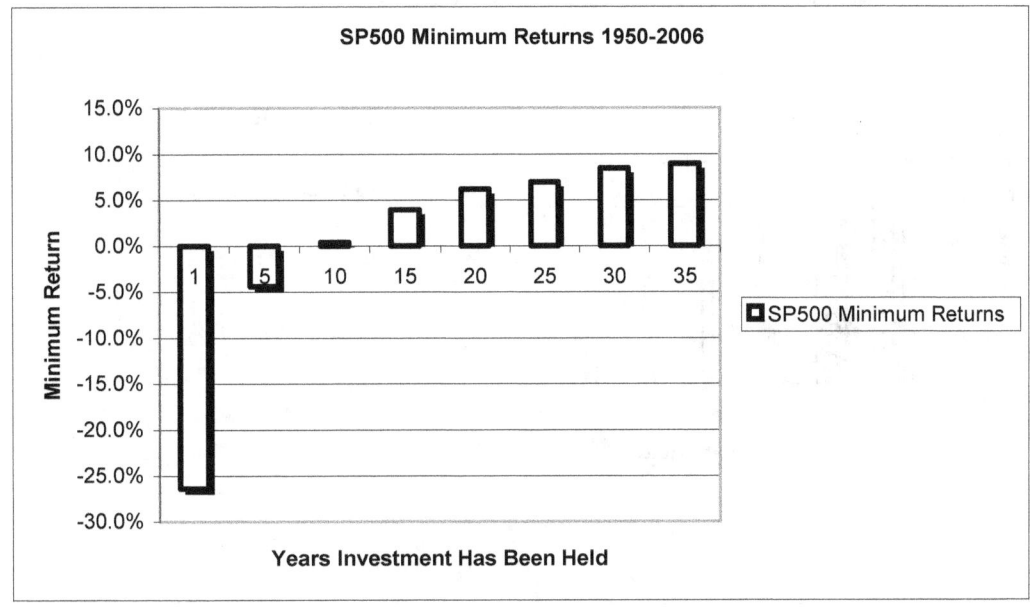

Years Held	SP500 Minimum Returns
1	-26.4%
5	-4.4%
10	0.4%
15	3.9%
20	6.2%
25	6.9%
30	8.5%
35	9.0%

Figure 13
S&P500 Minimum Returns 1950 To 2006

These statistics show that since 1950 the minimum return for any 30-year period from the S&P500 is 8.5%. Similarly, it is useful to know how many times in the past the S&P500 has returned less than a given amount as a function of the number of years the investment was held.

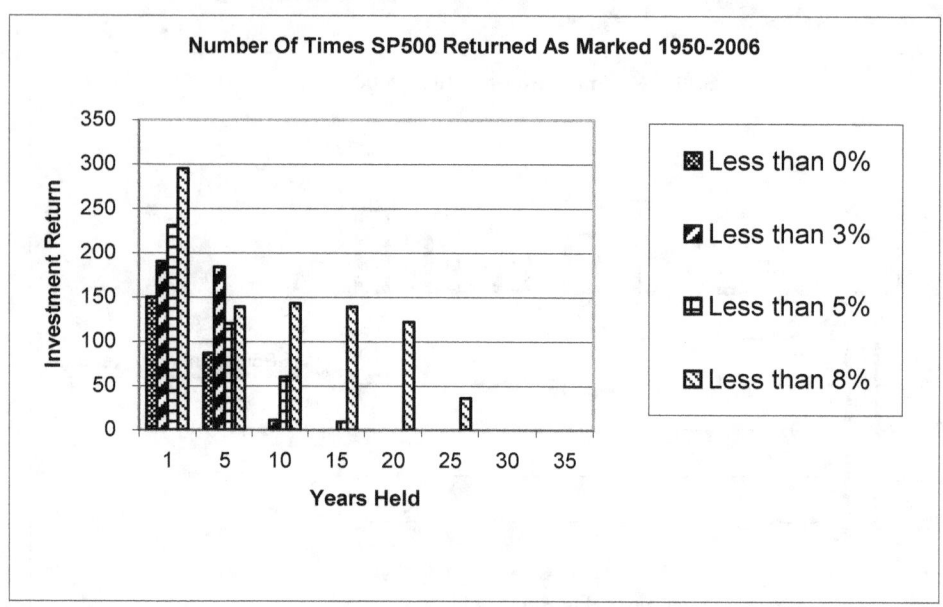

SP500 Occurrences 1950 - 2006 Return On Investment As Marked				
Period In Years	Less than 0%	Less than 3%	Less than 5%	Less than 8%
1	150	190	231	295
5	87	184	120	178
10	0	11	60	143
15	0	0	9	139
20	0	0	0	122
25	0	0	0	36
30	0	0	0	0
35	0	0	0	0

Figure 14
Occurrences Of Returns For S&P500

As in the previous graphic, these statistics also confirm that no 30-year period has returned less than 8% from the S&P500. Finally, these statistics can also be converted into percentages that approximate the probability of achieving a stated return for investments held a given number of years.

Investment Period In Years	SP500 Percent Of Occurrences 1950 - 2006 Return On Investment As Marked			
	Less than 0%	Less than 3%	Less than 5%	Less than 8%
1	22.69%	28.74%	34.95%	44.63%
5	14.48%	30.62%	19.97%	23.13%
10	0.00%	2.03%	11.09%	26.43%
15	0.00%	0.00%	1.87%	28.90%
20	0.00%	0.00%	0.00%	28.98%
25	0.00%	0.00%	0.00%	9.97%
30	0.00%	0.00%	0.00%	0.00%
35	0.00%	0.00%	0.00%	0.00%

Figure 15
Percentage Occurrences For S&P500

Time Is On Your Side

As in the "penny or million" example, time plays a crucial role in estimating the return on investment. The next two graphics home in on the expected long-term return on investment from the S&P500 and from an equity-indexed annuity capped at 9% and credited on a year-to-year basis.

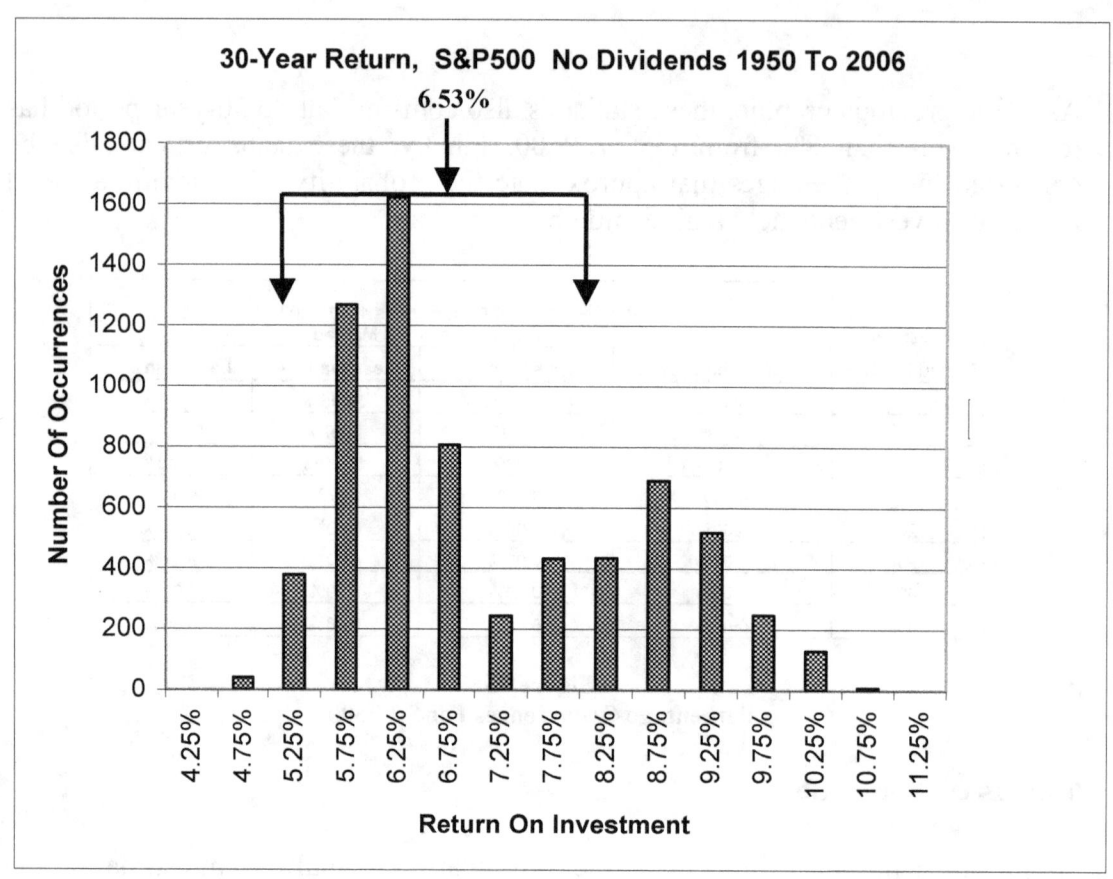

Figure 16
30-Year Return Distribution S&P500 1950 To 2007

Long-term investment in the S&P500 has rewarded the investor with an equivalent compound interest of almost 7% even without dividends. Reinvested dividends would add more than 3% to the total return. This compound return of about 10% is impressive considering the fact that it takes no thinking at all. It is nothing short of a loafer's dream!

An equity-indexed annuity held for the same 30 years yields the following results:

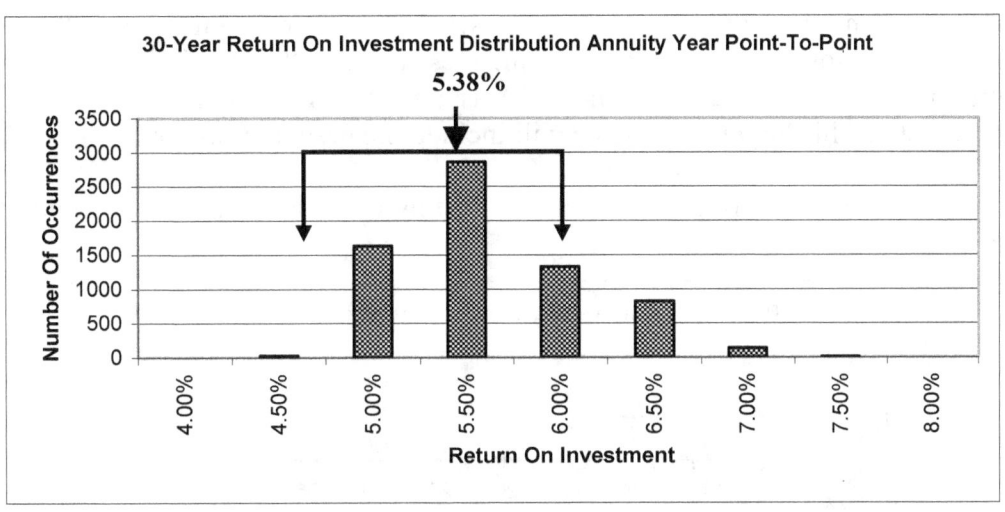

Figure 17
30-Year Return Distribution Annuity Year-To-Year Crediting Method

Investors who held an equity-indexed, capital protected annuity capped at a liberal 9% maximum yearly return would have earned an equivalent compound interest of 5.4%, or about half the return from the S&P500. Capital protection, it turns out, is very expensive.

The historical data concludes that investments that have been held for 30 years in the S&P500 since 1950 have never returned an equivalent compound interest lower than 8%. This is 4% higher than the average rate of inflation for the last 55 years. This observation highlights the importance of time in retirement financial planning. It is safe to say, then, that in our context, long-term means holding an investment course for at least 30 years.

The message is clear:

Start early, stay the course, and reinvest dividends!

The S&P500 does not extend beyond 1950; so, in a sense, it is biased toward positive results because it does not include the depression of 1929. It took over 20 years for the stock market to recover from the crash. The Dow Jones Index consists of 30 large companies and its history predates the Great Depression. It turns out that these two indices, the S&P500 and the Dow Jones Industrial Average, DJIA, behave very similarly. The statistical measurement for similarity between two sets of numbers is called the correlation. Two sets that are identical have a correlation value of 1.0; and two completely unrelated sets have a correlation value of 0.0. The correlation factor between the two indexes from 1950 to 2006 is 0.9949, suggesting that it possible to use the DJIA as a proxy for the S&P500 for the years 1928 to 2007. This larger time range will include the great depression.

Using the same analysis as in the S&P500, this extended time range yields the following results.

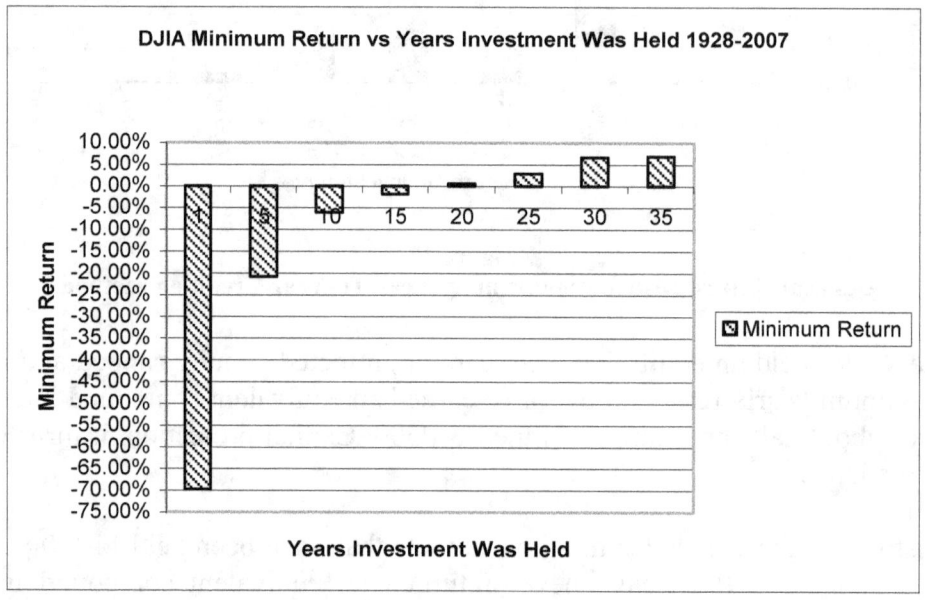

Years Held	Minimum Return DJIA 1928-2007
1	-69.76%
5	-20.82%
10	-6.04%
15	-1.86%
20	0.58%
25	2.92%
30	6.68%
35	6.94%

Figure 18
Dow Jones Average Minimum Returns

As with the S&P500, the longer period investment yields a higher return. No 30-year investment held in the DJIA, without dividends, since 1928 has yielded less than 6.68%, slightly less than the 8% returned by the S&P500 from 1950 to 2006, again with no dividends. The DJIA consists of only 30 companies, so it is not surprising that its actual return will differ from the S&P500.

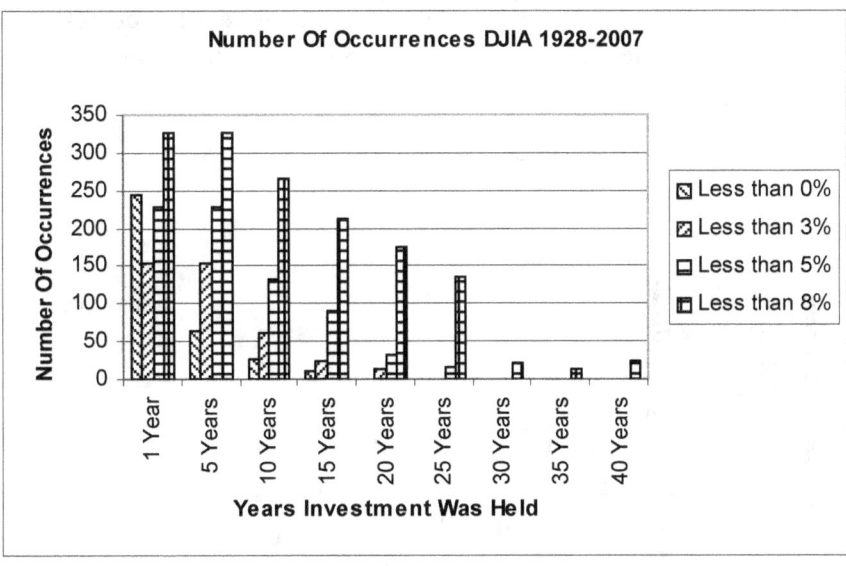

	Less than 0%	Less than 3%	Less than 5%	Less than 8%
1 Year	245	153	229	327
5 Years	64	153	229	327
10 Years	27	61	132	264
15 Years	11	24	89	213
20 Years	0	14	33	175
25 Years	0	1	16	135
30 Years	0	0	0	22
35 Years	0	0	0	12
40 Years	0	0	0	24

Figure 19
Dow Jones Average Statistics

The Great Depression of 1929 and its aftermath introduce 22 occurrences where a 30-year investment has yielded less than 8%; 18 of these occur before 1950.

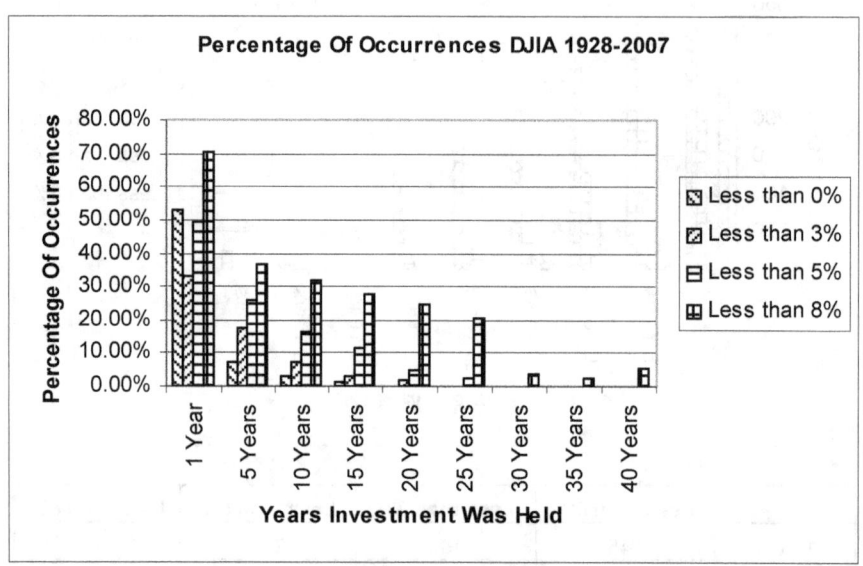

Investment Period	DJIA 1928 to 2007 Percentage Of Occurrences			
	Less than 0%	Less than 3%	Less than 5%	Less than 8%
1 Year	52.80%	32.97%	49.35%	70.47%
5 Years	7.24%	17.31%	25.90%	36.99%
10 Years	3.28%	7.40%	16.02%	32.04%
15 Years	1.44%	3.14%	11.65%	27.88%
20 Years	0.00%	1.99%	4.69%	24.86%
25 Years	0.00%	0.15%	2.44%	20.58%
30 Years	0.00%	0.00%	0.00%	3.77%
35 Years	0.00%	0.00%	0.00%	2.29%
40 Years	0.00%	0.00%	0.00%	5.17%

Figure 20
Dow Jones Average Occurrences

Now that the Great Depression is included in the data, the probability of a 30-year investment returning less than 8% rises to 3.77% for investments held between 1928 and 2007. Note that 82% of these occurrences happened before 1950.

The statistics above indicate that investing in the stock market involves risk—risk of losing capital as well as risk of earning less than expected. The investor demands a premium for this risk. The so-called equity-premium puzzle is that the stock market historically yields about 6% more than long-term government bonds. So, for example, if the long-term bonds have returned an average of 5%; the average stock market return over the long term has been about 11%, including dividends. Indeed, the S&P500 average 10-year return is about 11%.

The message still remains very clear:

Invest early, invest for the long term, and stay the course.

CHAPTER 6: THE FORK IN THE ROAD

You don't know who is swimming naked until the tide goes out.

There are only three components to retirement budget planning—savings, time and return on investment. The following chart summarizes the amount of savings needed to be set aside for retirement, using the following assumptions: 3% inflation rate, a current income of $46,326, the median household income in 2005, a goal of 80% of this budget at retirement, 35 working years left to retirement, and 25 years of retired living.

Required Yearly Savings	Return On Investment						
	3%	4%	5%	6%	7%	8%	9%
Without Social Security	$ 27,266	$20,996	$ 15,903	$ 12,152	$ 9,292	$ 7,024	$ 5,155
Percent Of Gross Income	59%	45%	34%	26%	20%	15%	11%
With 45% Contribution From Social Security	$ 11,929	$ 9,186	$ 6,957	$ 5,316	$ 4,065	$ 3,073	$ 2,255
Percent Of Gross Income	26%	20%	15%	11%	9%	7%	5%

The Social Security Administration estimates that its benefits will be about 45% of the retirement budget for this example. Without considering Social Security, the percentage of gross income required to meet the retirement objective varies from 59% to 11%. Depending on the return on investment, these requirements vary from the impossible to the doable. With Social Security added in, the percentages vary from 26% to 5% of gross income.

Using the average, annualized 10-year equivalent compound interest as a measurement standard, consider now the following table of average returns on investment:

Average Gross returns For A 10-Year Investment		
Inflation Protected Treasuries	Equity-indexed Annuities	S&P500 Funds
5%	5.5%	10.8%

Now it becomes clear that those investors who earn about 5% on their investments will have to set aside 15%-20% of their gross income to enjoy a retirement budget equal to 80% of their present one—an almost impossible task. This assumes that Social Security will continue to function as in the past, by no means guaranteed.

The point becomes abundantly clear that without the umbrella of Social Security, only those individuals earning 8% or more on investment will be able to meet their retirement financial goals and even they will have to set aside 10% to 15% of their gross income—a challenging task. Prudent planning suggests factoring in lower future Social Security benefits.

CHAPTER 7: KEEP IT SIMPLE

Momentum Investing: The fine art of buying high and selling low.
Value Investing: The art of buying low and selling lower.

The S&P500 index class of mutual funds and exchange-traded funds (ETFs) take the guess out of deciding which stocks or which class of stocks will perform best in any given year. Because of the popularity of index funds, a proliferation of exchange-traded funds has exploded in the investment world. Either traditional mutual funds or the new ETFs will do the same thing. The difference is that the ETF is traded like a stock so they are easier to place into existing brokerage accounts. ETFs may also have lower operating expenses and more favorable tax consequences than their mutual fund versions. With low expenses and a buffet of index funds to track everything from the S&P500 to small niche markets, ETFs are hard to resist. After all, we each view ourselves as better than average; so why not follow our instinct and invest in market sectors?

One place where it pays to be average is the stock market. The S&P500 index has beaten more than 75% of all professional money managers in the long term. Be average and beat most of the competition—a loafer's delight!

To illustrate the point, consider the next two graphs of the nine major stock market indices over the last 10 years:

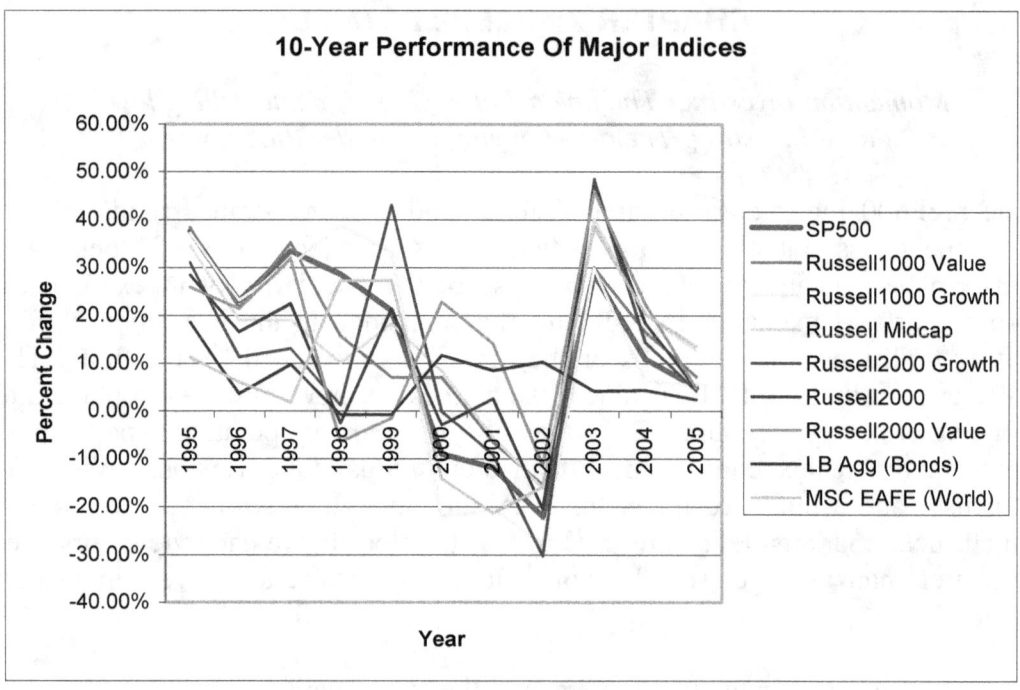

Figure 21
Stock Market Performance By Market Sector

The graph above illustrates that no single market index is consistently the top performer from year to year. Choosing a market sector on the basis of historical performance is like a dog chasing its own tail; it never catches up with it. So, if choosing the right market sector every time is impossible, why not invest equal amounts in all market sectors, a Composite index, and play all the odds?

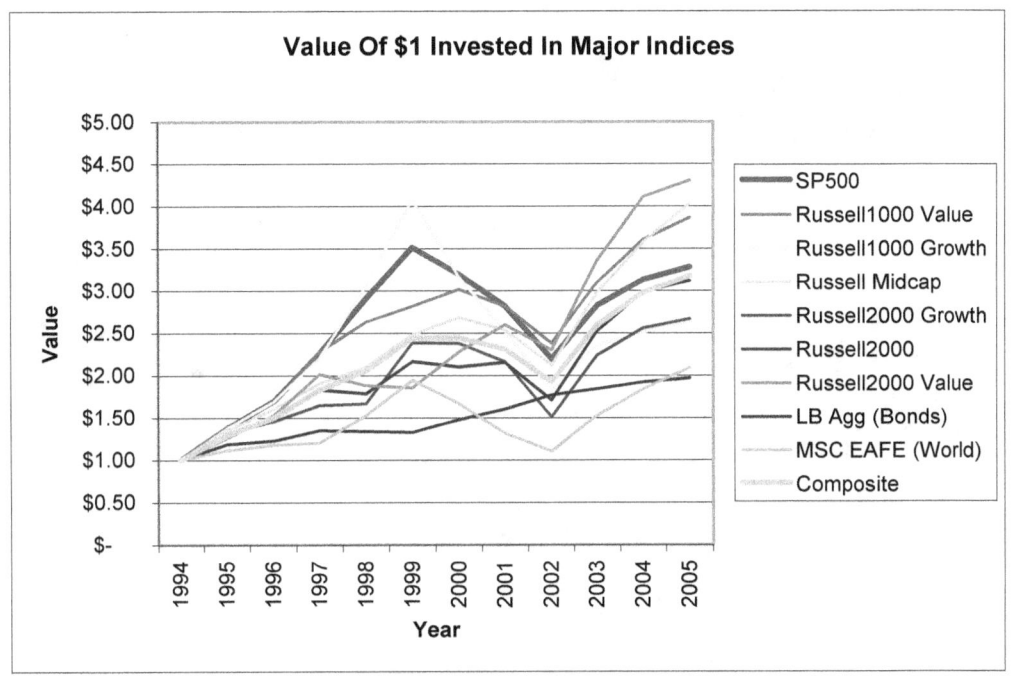

Figure 22
Value Of $1 Invested In Market Sectors

The second graph, Value Of $1 Invested In Major Indices, shows that a simple investment in the S&P500 outperformed the Composite over the last 10 years; and, in fact, outperformed six out of ten indices. From 1994 to 2001, for example, the S&P500 investment outperformed all others and may do so again.

The S&P500 index class of investment has the lowest expense ratio in the industry, giving greater value to the investor for every dollar invested. The message is simple; invest in the S&P500 and:

Keep It Simple!

CHAPTER 8: RISK OF RUIN

*An economist is someone who did not have
enough personality to become an accountant.*

Risk In The Accumulation Phase

The wealth accumulation phase of the life cycle requires the future retiree to seek an investment portfolio that returns at least 8%. There is a risk that the investment plan may not produce the hoped-for results. One method of estimating this risk is to compute the median and standard deviation for this class of investments. The median is defined as the value in the middle, half the values are greater and half the values are less than the median. Standard deviation is a measure of how spread out the data is about the median. 67% of all values fall within plus or minus one standard deviation.

This book promotes a 30-year investment in the SP500 index. The return characteristics for this class of investments are repeated below.

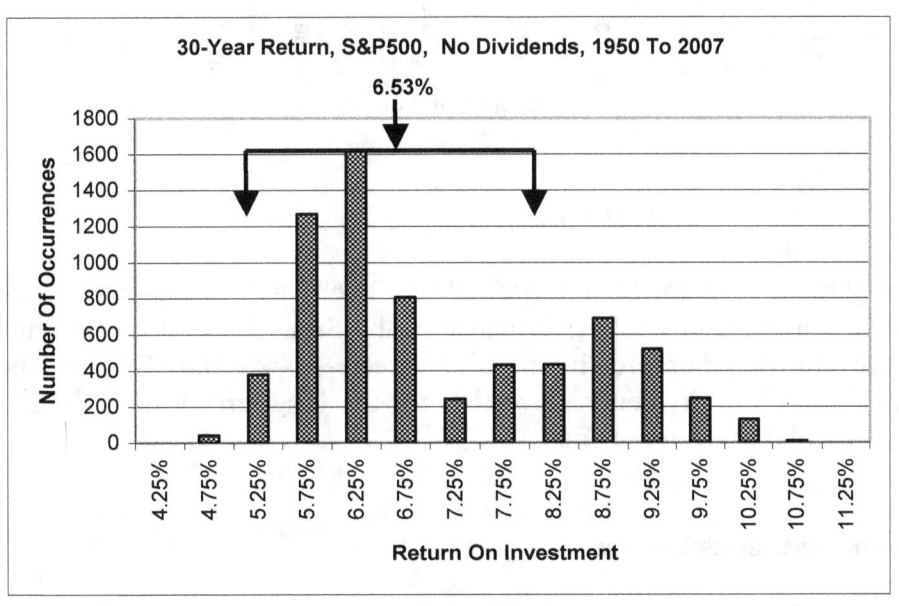

Figure 23
S&P500 Index 30-Year Return Statistics

The median return for the S&P500 index is 6.53% with a standard deviation of 1.39%. Adding the average yearly dividend of 3% means that the 30-year investor can expect a return of 9.53% with a spread of 1.39%. Putting it another way, the expected range of return before inflation for the 30-year investor is between 8.14% and 10.92% two times out of three.

Compare now the expected 30-year performance of the SP500 with its yearly counterpart repeated below:

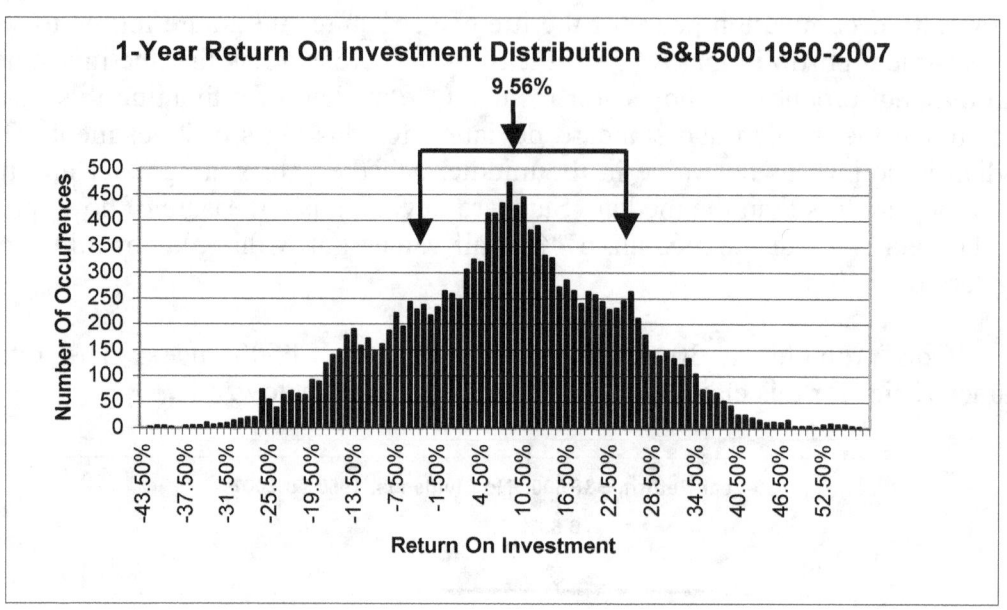

Figure 24
S&P500 Index 1-Year Return Statistics

The yearly median return for the S&P500 is 9.56% with a standard deviation of about 16%. The year-to-year performance of the S&P500 is much more uncertain because two times out of three it will fall between –3.44% and +28.56%, including an average of 3% in dividends. Investing for the long-term lowers the degree of uncertainty and thus decreases risk.

Risk In The Retirement Phase

Retirees face five risks: longevity risk, inflation risk, withdrawal rate risk, asset allocation risk, and health care expenditure risk. Only withdrawal and asset allocation risks are within the control of the retiree. The retirement phase consists of withdrawals as well as continuing investment. The risk of ruin is defined as the probability of running out of funds while still alive. Intuitively, a formula that computes the probability of retirement ruin must incorporate asset allocation risk in the form of median return on investment and standard deviation, withdrawal rates, and longevity. The retiree can control all variables but one, longevity or its inverse, mortality. Health care risk can be moderated with appropriate coverage. The chapters that follow outline a plan to reduce the risk of ruin to zero.

Risk Of Ruin

This section explains the mathematics behind the formula for Retirement Ruin; it may make interesting reading while smoking salmon or barbecuing spare ribs. Professor Moshe Milevsky of York University, Ontario, Canada, presents a very readable explanation in his paper, "A Gentle Introduction to the Calculus of Retirement Income: What is Your Retirement RisQuotient?"

In the opening section of his paper, Professor Milevsky writes:

"If a retiree is invested in a standard (balanced) portfolio and plans on withdrawing a fixed inflation-adjusted amount every year during retirement, he or she obviously faces the probability their portfolio will be exhausted while still alive. Under basic portfolio assumptions, the formula for this probability of retirement ruin – which is the probability that a fixed spending plan will deplete a retirement nest egg prior to the end of the lifecycle – can be expressed as follows:"

Risk of Ruin = Wealth is Zero & You Are Alive = $\dfrac{\displaystyle\int_{0}^{S/\beta} y^{(\alpha-1)} e^{-y} dy}{\displaystyle\int_{0}^{\infty} y^{(\alpha-1)} e^{-y} dy}$

$\alpha = (2(\mu + 2\lambda) \ / \ (\sigma^2 + \lambda)) - 1$

$\beta = (\sigma^2 + \lambda) / 2$

μ = Portfolio median rate of return

σ = Standard deviation of investment portfolio

λ = Mortality rate = $\ln(2)$ / Median Remaining Lifespan (MRL)

S= Inflation adjusted spending rate as a percentage of the retirement portfolio

$\ln(2) = 0.6934$

The mortality rate, λ, is derived by dividing the natural logarithm of 2, 0.693, by the median remaining lifespan, MRL. Given a certain age and sex of a retiree, half of that age population will live longer than the MRL, and half will live shorter than the MRL. Median Remaining Lifespan tables are available from the Social Security Administration and these values are plotted in Figure 25, Median Remaining Lifespan. α and β are explicit functions of the variables $\{\mu, \sigma, \lambda, S\}$.

Microsoft Excel can compute the Retirement Ruin formula above by invoking the following spreadsheet function:

Risk of Ruin = gammadist(S/β, α, 1, TRUE)

Excel will return a number equal to the percent probability of ruin given the inflation-adjusted median investment return, standard deviation, mortality, and spending rate.

For example: with an inflation adjusted S&P500 index portfolio return of 9.5%, a standard deviation of 16%, and a spending rate of 10% per year, a 65-year-old male retiree runs a 29% risk of running out of money while still alive.

Risk of Ruin = 29%

The retirees' portfolio investment risk, or standard deviation, is equal to the Standard and Poor's <u>one-year</u>, not 30-year, return standard deviation because yearly withdrawals come from the investment portfolio and the value of this portfolio can vary widely from year to year. Intuitively, withdrawals made during stock market downturns result in a smaller financial base. Market upturns, then, will result in smaller financial gains.

**Investment risk is greater in the withdrawal
stage than in the accumulation phase.**

The retiree can decrease his or her risk of ruin by decreasing the spending rate, increasing portfolio return or decreasing volatility, standard deviation. For example, if the same retiree reduces his spending rate from 10% to 4% a year his risk of ruin becomes:

Risk of Ruin = 1.77%

Chapter 13, *Weaving A Safety Net* and Chapter 14, *Guaranteed Income For Life*, explain how to reduce the mathematical risk of ruin to nearly zero.

Computation Of Retirement Ruin

Loafers with time on their hands, a calculator or spreadsheet, pencil, paper, and a cold beer may enjoy computing their own Risk of Ruin probability factor based on their personal portfolio. Use Figure 25, Median Remaining Lifespan, to find your personal MRL, then compute λ, α, and β. Finally, use Figure 26, Risk of Ruin table to find the factor that approximates the risk of ruin.

Example:

λ = Female, 65 years old (MRL =18.4) = ln(2) / 18.4 = 0.03766
μ = Inflation-adjusted portfolio median rate of return = 8%
σ = Standard deviation of investment portfolio = 15%
S= Inflation adjusted spending rate as a percentage of the retirement portfolio =6%
ln(2)=0.6934

Compute:

$$\alpha = (2(\mu + 2\lambda) \ / (\sigma^2 + \lambda)) - 1 = \ 4.163$$

$$\beta = (\sigma^2 + \lambda) / 2 \ = \ .030085$$

$$S \ / \ \beta \ = \ 1.994$$

From Figure 26, Risk of Ruin, along the "Beta Adjusted Spending Rate" row on top find the number that is just greater than 1.994. The number is 2.0. Move down the 2.0 column until reaching the Alpha row with the number that is just smaller than 4.163 (the number is 4.1), the percentage value where the column and row intersect is the approximate risk of ruin.

Risk of Ruin = 13.0%

Sometime values of α and β will be off the chart. When this happens, simply extrapolate from the last value available; this is, after all, only an estimate.

Readers who fear they may exhaust their beer supply before completing all calculations are invited to visit the Loafer's free interactive web-based spreadsheet:

http://mysite.verizon.net/geode/loafer.xls

where the computation of risk of ruin is just a few clicks away.

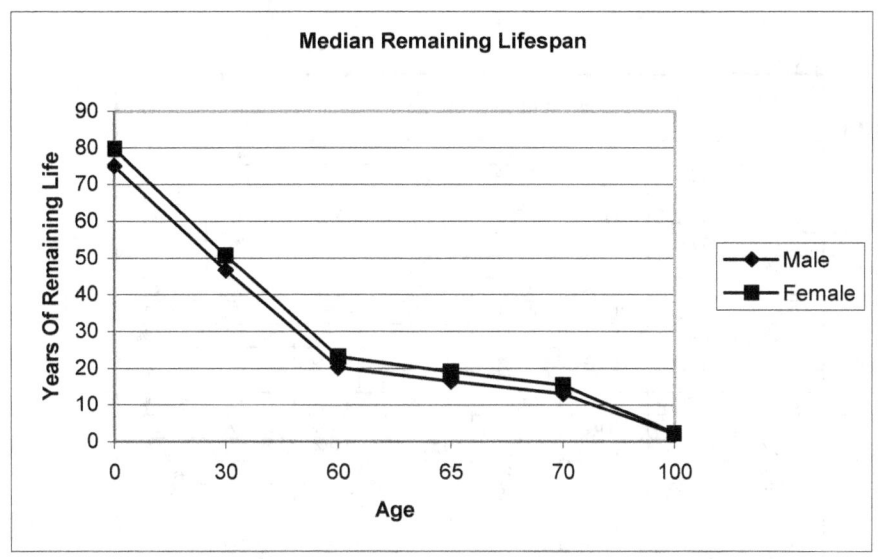

Figure 25
Median Remaining Lifespan

Alpha	Beta Adjusted Spending Rate							
	0.5	0.65	0.8	0.95	1.1	1.25	1.4	1.55
4.5	0.1%	0.2%	0.4%	0.7%	1.2%	1.9%	2.8%	4.0%
4.3	0.1%	0.2%	0.5%	1.0%	1.6%	2.5%	3.7%	5.1%
4.1	0.1%	0.4%	0.8%	1.4%	2.2%	3.3%	4.7%	6.4%
3.9	0.2%	0.5%	1.1%	1.9%	3.0%	4.4%	6.1%	8.1%
3.7	0.3%	0.8%	1.5%	2.6%	4.0%	5.7%	7.7%	10.1%
3.5	0.5%	1.2%	2.1%	3.5%	5.2%	7.3%	9.7%	12.4%
3.3	0.8%	1.7%	3.0%	4.7%	6.8%	9.3%	12.1%	15.3%
3.1	1.2%	2.4%	4.1%	6.2%	8.8%	11.7%	15.0%	18.5%
2.9	1.8%	3.4%	5.5%	8.2%	11.3%	14.7%	18.4%	22.3%
2.7	2.6%	4.7%	7.4%	10.6%	14.3%	18.2%	22.4%	26.7%
2.5	3.7%	6.5%	9.9%	13.7%	17.9%	22.4%	26.9%	31.5%
2.3	5.4%	8.9%	13.0%	17.5%	22.2%	27.1%	32.1%	36.9%
2.1	7.6%	12.0%	16.9%	22.0%	27.3%	32.6%	37.8%	42.8%
1.9	10.6%	16.0%	21.6%	27.4%	33.1%	38.7%	44.0%	49.1%
1.7	14.7%	21.0%	27.3%	33.6%	39.6%	45.3%	50.7%	55.6%
1.5	19.9%	27.1%	34.1%	40.7%	46.8%	52.5%	57.7%	62.4%
1.3	26.5%	34.4%	41.8%	48.5%	54.5%	60.0%	64.8%	69.1%
1.1	34.7%	43.1%	50.5%	56.9%	62.6%	67.6%	71.9%	75.6%

Alpha	Beta Adjusted Spending Rate							
	1.7	1.85	2	2.15	2.3	2.45	2.6	2.75	2.9
4.5	5.4%	7.0%	8.9%	10.9%	13.2%	15.7%	18.3%	21.1%	24.0%
4.3	6.7%	8.6%	10.8%	13.1%	15.7%	18.4%	21.3%	24.3%	27.4%
4.1	8.4%	10.6%	13.0%	15.7%	18.5%	21.5%	24.6%	27.8%	31.1%
3.9	10.3%	12.9%	15.6%	18.6%	21.7%	24.9%	28.3%	31.6%	35.0%
3.7	12.7%	15.6%	18.6%	21.9%	25.2%	28.7%	32.2%	35.7%	39.2%
3.5	15.4%	18.6%	22.0%	25.5%	29.1%	32.8%	36.4%	40.1%	43.7%
3.3	18.6%	22.2%	25.8%	29.6%	33.4%	37.2%	41.0%	44.7%	48.3%
3.1	22.3%	26.1%	30.1%	34.0%	38.0%	41.9%	45.7%	49.4%	53.0%
2.9	26.4%	30.5%	34.7%	38.8%	42.9%	46.8%	50.6%	54.3%	57.8%
2.7	31.0%	35.4%	39.7%	43.9%	48.0%	51.9%	55.7%	59.3%	62.6%
2.5	36.1%	40.7%	45.1%	49.3%	53.3%	57.2%	60.8%	64.2%	67.4%
2.3	41.7%	46.3%	50.7%	54.8%	58.8%	62.5%	65.9%	69.1%	72.0%
2.1	47.6%	52.2%	56.5%	60.5%	64.2%	67.7%	70.8%	73.8%	76.4%
1.9	53.8%	58.2%	62.3%	66.1%	69.6%	72.7%	75.6%	78.2%	80.6%
1.7	60.2%	64.4%	68.2%	71.6%	74.8%	77.6%	80.1%	82.4%	84.4%
1.5	66.6%	70.4%	73.9%	76.9%	79.6%	82.1%	84.2%	86.1%	87.8%
1.3	72.9%	76.3%	79.2%	81.8%	84.1%	86.2%	87.9%	89.5%	90.8%
1.1	78.9%	81.7%	84.2%	86.3%	88.2%	89.8%	91.2%	92.4%	93.4%

Figure 26
Risk of Ruin

CHAPTER 9: A TALE OF THREE FAMILIES

*We have two classes of forecasters: Those who don't
know and those who don't know they don't know!*

Meet three families: the Andersons, the Browns, and the Caldwells. Each family consists of a wife and a husband (all are 30 years old) and each family has two children. They live in Median, USA, where every household earns $46,326, the median U.S. income for 2005. As employees, they all pay Social Security taxes, set money aside for the children's future educations, have a zero or negative savings rate, and do not contribute to the company retirement plan.

All three households intend to work until age 65 and plan on at least one spouse surviving until age 90. Their financial plans are all the same in that they plan on a household retirement budget equal to 81% of their present expenses (in today's dollars).

This assumption is probably reasonable in that they should own their home free and clear, education costs for the children will be a thing of the past, and Medicare will temper medical expenses. In addition, these couples should be able to pay cash for automobiles, as needed, without incurring a fixed monthly payment.

All three families are keenly aware of the eroding effect of inflation, so they plan on an inflation rate of 3% per year. This rate is slightly below the historical average, but major expense components of the CPI, like housing, will be reduced and income taxes may be lower. Also, Social Security payments are inflation indexed and, as stated above, Medicare will temper medical expenses.

Finally, the Social Security Administration estimates that Social Security will provide about 46% of their retirement budget. The three families must then provide for the remaining 35% to equal 81% of current expenses. They each plan to make yearly contributions to their private retirement nest eggs, even if that means reducing some of their other expenses.

Their first task is to determine the future value of their present budget. To do this they use the Future Value Table, Table 1 in *Appendix 1*, 35 years to retirement and 3% inflation.

The future value of the $46,326 budget is 2.81 greater than today's or:

Budget in 35 years = 46,326 x 2.81 = $130,176 per year.

Since each household plans on budgeting for 25 years of retirement that will increase yearly at the rate of inflation, they will need:

Total Retirement Funds = $4,732,094

Each household will need to have 35% of this amount at the time of retirement, or:

Funds Needed At Retirement = $1,656,233

In present dollars this amount is $588,598. After recovering from shock, each family decides on a different course. The Andersons are very conservative and they are happy just keeping up with inflation by investing in CD's or money market at the current after tax rate of 3%.

The Browns, although conservative, know that they can earn about two percentage points above inflation by investing in U.S. treasuries such as TIPS, treasury inflation protected securities. Their expected return on investment is 5%.

The Caldwells decide to invest in low cost exchange traded funds or mutual funds focused on a market index, such as the S&P500. Historically, the S&P500 has yielded double-digit returns over the long term; but, being cautious, the Caldwells assume an 8% return on investment over their 35 working years. This decision is based on their observation that, historically, no 35-year investment period in the S&P500 has yielded less than 8%.

Each household will retain the same investment strategy during their retirement years, dollar cost averaging their withdrawals just as they did during their saving phase. Dollar cost averaging means regularly adding to or withdrawing from an investment account, such as an S&P500 index fund, regardless of the value of the S&P500. Next, each family must determine how much to contribute to their private nest egg in order to meet their retirement goals. If income rises at a rate higher than inflation, the extra income can be used to increase savings, enhance the standard of living, or both.

Here is how each family computes their first annual contribution:

The details of the computations are explained in Chapter 10, *The Caldwell Retirement Budget Planner*. Using Table 2, in *Appendix 1*, at the intersection of 35 years to retirement and 25 years of retirement, the Andersons find a factor of 0.7357, to compute their first annual payment:

First Anderson Annual Payment = $46,326 x 0.35 x 0.7357 x 1 = $11,929

Tables 2 is the same for all three families, but the Browns use the 5% column in Tables 3 and 8, and derive a factor of 0.5832, to compute their first annual payment:

First Brown Annual Payment = $46,326 x 0.35 x 0.7357 x 0.5832 = $6,957

Similarly, the Caldwells use the 8% column in Tables 3 and 8, *Appendix 1*, and derive a factor of 0.2576, to compute their first annual payment:

First Caldwell Annual Payment = $46,326 x 0.35 x 0.7357 x 0.2576 =$3,073

These savings contributions to the retirement fund will need to increase at the rate of inflation each year. The factors appear in Table 1 under the 3% column. For the Andersons, the amount required represents about 26% of their gross income—an impossible objective. The Brown's contribution represents an equally daunting 15% of their income. The Caldwells, however, face a required savings rate of just 7%, a realizable goal, especially if they take advantage of their company's matching program in the retirement plan. In fact, all they have to do is contribute 4% of their income to the retirement plan and the company will match it with another 4%. Done! Here is how the percentage of required savings compares:

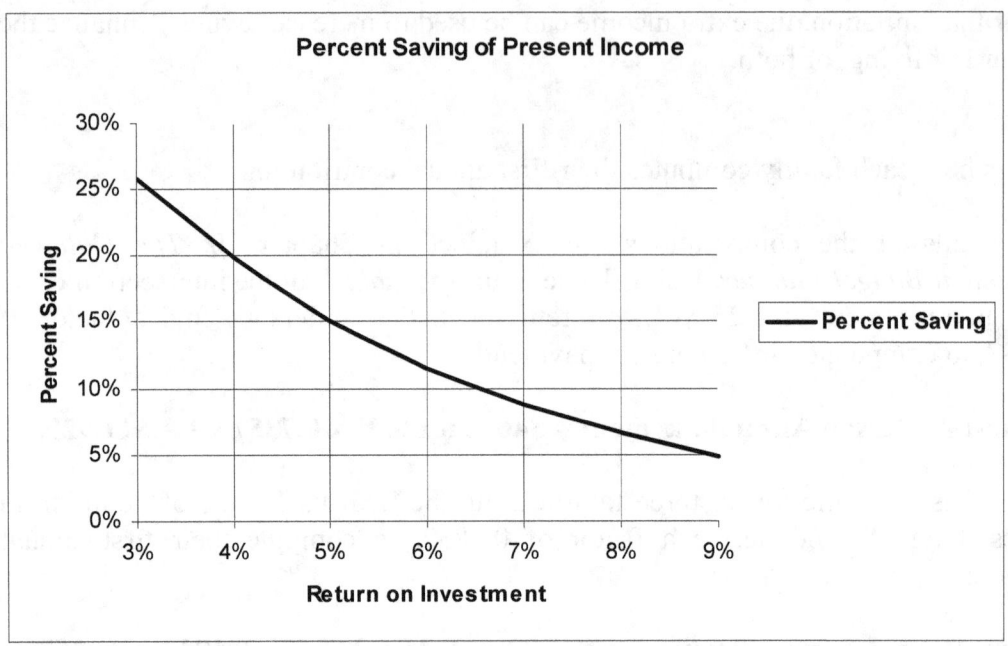

Figure 27
Percent Saving Of Present Income

The required contribution to the retirement fund decreases with increasing return on investment. Let's follow the families through their saving years:

Years to Retirement	The Saving Years		
	Anderson	Brown	Caldwell
35	$ 11,929	$ 6,957	$ 3,073
34	$ 24,574	$ 14,472	$ 6,484
33	$ 37,966	$ 22,576	$ 10,262
32	$ 52,140	$ 31,308	$ 14,441
31	$ 67,131	$ 40,704	$ 19,055
30	$ 82,974	$ 50,805	$ 24,142
29	$ 99,706	$ 61,652	$ 29,742
28	$ 117,369	$ 73,292	$ 35,901
27	$ 136,001	$ 85,770	$ 42,666
26	$ 155,646	$ 99,136	$ 50,088
25	$ 176,347	$ 113,444	$ 58,225
24	$ 198,149	$ 128,746	$ 67,137
23	$ 221,102	$ 145,103	$ 76,889
22	$ 245,253	$ 162,576	$ 87,553
21	$ 270,654	$ 181,229	$ 99,205
20	$ 297,359	$ 201,129	$ 111,929
19	$ 325,422	$ 222,351	$ 125,814
18	$ 354,901	$ 244,968	$ 140,958
17	$ 385,856	$ 269,061	$ 157,466
16	$ 418,350	$ 294,714	$ 175,452
15	$ 452,445	$ 322,016	$ 195,038
14	$ 488,210	$ 351,059	$ 216,357
13	$ 525,713	$ 381,943	$ 239,554
12	$ 565,027	$ 414,772	$ 264,783
11	$ 606,227	$ 449,654	$ 292,212
10	$ 649,391	$ 486,704	$ 322,023
9	$ 694,598	$ 526,043	$ 354,411
8	$ 741,934	$ 567,800	$ 389,590
7	$ 791,484	$ 612,108	$ 427,788
6	$ 843,340	$ 659,109	$ 469,252
5	$ 897,595	$ 708,952	$ 514,251
4	$ 954,346	$ 761,794	$ 563,074
3	$ 1,013,695	$ 817,800	$ 616,032
2	$ 1,075,745	$ 877,144	$ 673,465
1	$ 1,140,606	$ 940,008	$ 735,737

Figure 28
Three Families The Saving Years

Of the three, the Caldwells are the only ones likely to save the required amount. The table, nonetheless, tracks the saving account of each family as if each were able to follow the plan. At retirement, the Caldwells will have $735,737 to see them through their golden years.

Next, let's follow the families through their retirement years.

Years of Retirement	The Retirement Years		
	Anderson	Brown	Caldwell
1	$ 1,127,831	$ 939,103	$ 745,322
2	$ 1,113,264	$ 936,715	$ 754,195
3	$ 1,096,807	$ 932,728	$ 762,256
4	$ 1,078,360	$ 927,017	$ 769,393
5	$ 1,057,820	$ 919,450	$ 775,486
6	$ 1,035,077	$ 909,887	$ 780,403
7	$ 1,010,017	$ 898,180	$ 783,999
8	$ 982,522	$ 884,171	$ 786,118
9	$ 952,469	$ 867,694	$ 786,588
10	$ 919,728	$ 848,573	$ 785,224
11	$ 884,165	$ 826,621	$ 781,821
12	$ 845,640	$ 801,640	$ 776,160
13	$ 804,009	$ 773,420	$ 768,000
14	$ 759,118	$ 741,740	$ 757,079
15	$ 710,811	$ 706,366	$ 743,113
16	$ 658,922	$ 667,049	$ 725,795
17	$ 603,279	$ 623,527	$ 704,788
18	$ 543,706	$ 575,523	$ 679,728
19	$ 480,014	$ 522,743	$ 650,221
20	$ 412,012	$ 464,878	$ 615,836
21	$ 339,498	$ 401,599	$ 576,108
22	$ 262,262	$ 332,561	$ 530,532
23	$ 180,087	$ 257,397	$ 478,560
24	$ 92,745	$ 175,722	$ 419,598
25	$ 0	$ 87,126	$ 353,002

Figure 29
Three Families The Retirement Years

Each account shrinks toward zero after 25 years of retirement. The factors used in the tables are designed to result in a small surplus at the end of the target period. Clearly, this book uses a draw-down approach to retirement financing; that is, the retirement account is reduced to nearly zero at the maximum age of survival. Families who wish to leave a legacy for their children will need a larger retirement account or a more modest life-style.

CHAPTER 10: THE CALDWELL RETIREMENT BUDGET PLANNER

In order to determine the amount of the first year payment the Caldwells need to fill out the Retirement Budget Planner. Each line of the planner is explained in detail here.

Line 1
Enter the total present budget, including income taxes, $46,326

Line 2
Enter years to retirement, 35

Line 3
Enter years of longest retirement, 25

Line 4
Enter Your Age 30

Line 5
Enter Rate of Inflation (3% or 4%) 3%

Line 6
Enter Desired Percent Of Total Budget For Retirement 0.81

Line 7
Enter Targeted Return On Investment 8%

Line 8
Future Value Factor, Table 1, Int. Of 35 With 3% Inflation 2.8139

Line 9
Future Tot. Ret. Budget Factor (Table 4, int. of 35 with 8%) 239.43

Line 10
First Payment Factor (Table 2, intersection of 35 years to and 25 of retirement) 0.7357

Line 11
Multiplication Factor Table 3 (for 3% inflation), int. of 35 and 8%) 0.3994

Line 12
Table 8, intersection of 25 years of retirement and 8%. 0.62

Line 13
Line 11 x Line 12 + 0.01 0.2576

Line 14
Future Value Factor For Existing Funds (Table 1 Intersection of 35 and 8%) 14.7853

Line 15
Total Percent Contribution To Company Retirement Plan 0%

Line 16
Budget In Future Dollars (Line 1 x Line 8) $130,357

Line 17
Future Budget Factor (Line 10 x Line 13 x Line 16) $24,705

Line 18
Total Future Value Of Budget (Line 9 x Line 17) $ 5,915,118

Line 19
Present Value Of All Tax Deferred Accounts $0

Line 20
Future Value Of All Tax Deferred Accounts (Line 14 x Line 19) $0

Line 21
Total Yearly Contributions to Retirement Plan (Line 1 x Line 15) $ 0
Line 22
Future Value Of Retirement Plans (Line 9 x Line 21) $ 0
Line 23
Savings $ 0
Line 24
Future Value Of Savings (Line 14 x Line 23) $ 0
Line 25
Total Future Values From Retirement Plan and Savings (Line 20 + Line 22 + Line 24) $ 0
Line 26
Fractional Reduction (Line 25/Line 18)   0.0
Line 27
Yearly Social Security Payment In Future Dollars (from SS Administration) $59,796
Line 28
Fractional Reduction (Line 27/Line16)   0.46
Line 29
1.0 - Line 6   0.19
Line 30
Sum (L26 + L28+L29)   0.65
Line 31
1.0 - Line 30   0.35
Line 32
Budget to finance (Line 1 x Line 31) $16,214
Line 33
Yearly Payment (Line 10 x Line 13 x Line 32) $3,073

$3,073 is the first yearly payment the Caldwells must make into their retirement fund. If the Caldwells increase their payments by their assumed inflation rate of 3% each year, and invest all their funds at an average rate of 8% per year, they will meet all the requirements to fund 25 years of retirement.

Caldwell Risk Of Ruin

The Caldwells remain fully vested in the S&P500 index throughout their retirement. The one-year inflation adjusted total return (inflation=3%) of the S&P500 is about 9.5%; the standard deviation is about 15%, the higher MRL is 22 (the wife's). Their retirement nest egg at 65 will be $735,737 (Figure 28, last line) and the inflation-adjusted withdrawals at age 65 will be $45,624 (Figure 36, Line 1-Column 2; the Caldwell withdrawal is the same as that of the Efland). The spending rate, S, is then 6.2%, $45,624 divided by $735,737. Their probability of running out of funds while still alive is about:

Risk of Ruin(Caldwell) = 13%

	The Caldwell Budget Planner				
1	Budget In Today's Dollars				$ 46,326
2	Years To Retirement	35			
3	Longest Years Of Retirement	25			
4	Enter Your Age	30			
5	Inflation Factor (3% or 4%)	3%			
6	Desired Fraction Of Total Budget	0.81			
7	Target Return On Investments	8%			
8	Future Value Factor From Table 1 (Intersection of 35 years and 3%)	2.8139			
9	Future Total Retirement Budget Factor (Table 4 intersection of 35 years and 8%)	239.430			
10	First Payment Factor (Table 2 intersection of 35 years to and 25 years of retirement)	0.7357			
11	Multiplication Factor (Table 3 (for 3% inflation) intersection of 8% and 35 yrs to ret.)	0.3994			
12	Table 8 (for 3%) Intersection of 8% and 25 years of retirement	0.62			
13	Line 11 x Line 12 + .01	0.2576			
14	Future Value Factor For Existing Funds (Table 1 intersection of 35 and 8%)	14.7853			
15	Total Percent Contribution To Company Retirement Plan	0%			
16	Budget In Future Dollars (Line 1 x Line 8)		$ 130,357		
	Initial Computation Of Required Yearly Contributions				
17	Future Budget Factor (Line 10 x Line 13 x Line 16)		$ 24,705		
18	Total Future Value Of Budget (Line 9 x Line 17)			$ 5,915,118	
	Compute Impact Of All Present Savings And Retirement Plans				
19	Present Value Of All Tax Deferred Accounts	$ 0			
20	Future Value Of All Tax Deferred Accounts (Line 14 x Line 19)		$ 0		
21	Total Yearly Contributions to Retirement Plan (Line 1 x Line 15)	$ 0			
22	Future Value Of Retirement Plans (Line 9 x Line 21)		$ 0		
23	Savings	$ 0			
24	Future Value Of Savings (Line 14 x Line 23)		$ 0		
25	Total Future Values From Retirement Plan and Savings (Line 20+ Line 22 + Line 24)			$ 0	
26	Fractional Reduction (Line 25/Line 18)		0.0		
	Compute Impact Of Future Social Security Payments				
27	Yearly Social Security Payment In Future Dollars from Social Security Administration		$ 59,796		
28	Fractional Reduction (Line 27/Line16)		0.46		
29	1.0 - Line 6		0.19		
30	Sum (L 26 + L 28 + L 29)		0.65		
31	1.0 - Line 30		0.35		
32	Budget to finance (Line 1 x Line 31)				$ 16,214
	Compute Yearly Payment To Meet Retirement Budget				
33	**Yearly Payment** (Line 10 x Line 13 x Line 32)				$ 3,073

Figure 30
The Caldwell Budget Planner

The parameters used to develop the Caldwell retirement budget are designed with built-in safety factors that reduce the probability of depleting all funds while still alive. These factors work to reduce the probability of financial ruin to about 10%.

CHAPTER 11: THE DALE TALE

A market analyst is an expert who will know tomorrow
why the things he predicted yesterday didn't happen.

Meet the Dales; they too live in Median, USA. Their family income is $46,326; but, being 50 years old, they look forward to retiring in 15 years. Unlike their younger neighbors, they participate in their company's tax deferred savings plan contributing 6% of their income. The company matches their contribution so their total savings amount to 12% annually. The value of their company savings plan is now $160,000, about double the national average. The Dales also have a savings account of $5,000. Being conservative, they choose a guaranteed income plan that has delivered an average 6% return on their investment. They plan to stay in this investment plan.

They would like to retire on about 80% of their present income and want to know if they are well poised to meet this objective or if they need to put aside additional savings. Alternatively, they want to know what budget they can expect to maintain in their retirement years if they cannot afford to save any more than they already do.

They fill out their budget retirement planner as follows:

	The Dale Budget Planner				
1	Budget In Today's Dollars				$ 46,326
2	Years To Retirement	15			
3	Longest Years Of Retirement	25			
4	Your Age	50			
5	Inflation Factor (3% or 4%)	3%			
6	Desired Fraction Of Total Budget	0.80			
7	Target Return On Investments	6%			
8	Future Value Factor From Table 1 (Intersection of 15 years and 3%)	1.558			
9	Future Total Retirement Budget Factor (Table 4 intersection of 15 years and 6%)	27.9530			
10	First Payment Factor (Table 2 intersection of 15 years to and 25 years of retirement)	1.7167			
11	Multiplication Factor (Table 3 (for 3% inflation) intersection of 6% and 15 yrs to ret.)	0.8117			
12	Table 8 (for 3%) Intersection of 6% and 25 years of retirement	0.74			
13	Line 11 x Line 12 + .01	0.611			
14	Future Value Factor For Existing Funds (Table 1 intersection of 15 and 6%)	2.3966			
15	Total Percent Contribution To Company Retirement Plan	12%			
16	Budget In Future Dollars (Line 1 x Line 8)		$ 72,176		
	Initial Computation Of Required Yearly Contributions				
17	Future Budget Factor (Line 10 x Line 13 x Line 16)		$ 75,706		
18	Total Future Value Of Budget (Line 9 x Line 17)			$ 2,116,210	
	Compute Impact Of All Present Savings And Retirement Plans				
19	Present Value Of All Tax Deferred Accounts	$ 160,000			
20	Future Value Of All Tax Deferred Accounts (Line 14 x Line 19)		$ 383,456		
21	Total Yearly Contributions to Retirement Plan (Line 1 x Line 15)	$ 5,559			
22	Future Value Of Retirement Plans (Line 9 x Line 21)		$ 155,391		
23	Savings	$ 5,000			
24	Future Value Of Savings (Line 14 x Line 23)		$ 11,983		
25	Total Future Values From Retirement Plan and Savings (Line 20+ Line 22 + Line 24)			$ 550,830	
26	Fractional Reduction (Line 25/Line 18)		0.26		
	Compute Impact Of Future Social Security Payments				
27	Yearly Social Security Payment In Future Dollars from Social Security Administration		$ 26,760		
28	Fractional Reduction (Line 27/Line16)		0.37		
29	1.0 - Line 6		0.20		
30	Sum (L 26 + L 28 + L 29)		0.83		
31	1.0 - Line 30		0.17		
32	Budget to finance (Line 1 x Line 31)				$ 7,875
	Compute Yearly Payment To Meet Retirement Budget				
33	Yearly Payment (Line 10 x Line 13 x Line 32)				$ 8,260

Figure 31 Version 1
The Dale Budget Planner

Because the Dales do not have as many years left to accumulate wealth, the built-in safety parameters force the Dales to set aside extra financial padding to protect them in case their investment plans do not go as planned. The Dales now realize that they need to inject an additional $8,260 per year, increased yearly for inflation, into their retirement fund if they are to meet their budget goal. Alternatively, they can settle for a retired life-style that is 63% of their present one without increasing their saving rate. Figure 31 Version 2 illustrates this strategy by changing Line 6 from 0.80 to 0.63 as the fraction of present budget.

	The Dale Budget Planner Version 2					
1	Budget In Today's Dollars					$ 46,326
2	Years To Retirement	15				
3	Longest Years Of Retirement	25				
4	Age	50				
5	Inflation Factor (3% or 4%)	3%				
6	Desired Fraction Of Total Budget	0.63				
7	Target Return On Investments	6%				
8	Future Value Factor From Table 1 (Intersection of 15 years and 3%)	1.558				
9	Future Total Retirement Budget Factor (Table 4 intersection of 35 years and 6%)	27.9530				
10	First Payment Factor (Table 2 intersection of 35 years to and 15 years of retirement)	1.7167				
11	Multiplication Factor (Table3 (for 3% inflation) intersection of 6% and 15 yrs to ret.)	0.8117				
12	Table 8 (for 3%) Intersection of 6% and 25 years of retirement	0.74				
13	Line 11 x Line 12 + .01	0.611				
14	Future Value Factor For Existing Funds (Table 1 intersection of 35 and 6%)	2.3966				
15	Total Percent Contribution To Company Retirement Plan	12%				
16	Budget In Future Dollars (Line 1 x Line 8)		$ 72,176			
	Initial Computation Of Required Yearly Contributions					
17	Future Budget Factor (Line 10 x Line 13 x Line 16)		$ 75,706			
18	Total Future Value Of Budget (Line 9 x Line 17)			$ 2,116,210		
	Compute Impact Of All Present Savings And Retirement Plans					
19	Present Value Of All Tax Deferred Accounts	$ 160,000				
20	Future Value Of All Tax Deferred Accounts (Line 14 x Line 19)		$ 383,456			
21	Total Yearly Contributions to Retirement Plan (Line 1 x Line15)	$ 5,559				
22	Future Value Of Retirement Plans (line 9 x Line 21)		$ 155,391			
23	Savings	$ 5,000				
24	Future Value Of Savings (Line 14 x Line 23)		$ 11,983			
25	Total Future Values From Retirement Plan and Savings (Line20+ Line 22 + Line 24)			$ 550,830		
26	Fractional Reduction (Line 25/Line 18)		0.26			
	Compute Impact Of Future Social Security Payments					
27	Yearly Social Security Payment In Future Dollars from Social Security Administration		$ 26,760			
28	Fractional Reduction (Line 27/Line 16)		0.37			
29	1.0 - Line 6		0.37			
30	Sum (L 26 + L 28+L 29)		1.00			
31	1.0 - Line 30		0.00			
32	Budget to finance (Line 1 x Line 31)					$ 0
	Compute Yearly Payment To Meet Retirement Budget					
33	**Yearly Payment** (Line 10 x Line 13 x Line 32)					**$ 0**

**Figure 31 Version 2
The Dale Budget Planner**

Now that the Dales know their alternatives they can decide on a course of action that is proper for them, perhaps a smaller injection of funds and a more modest lifestyle.

CHAPTER 12: SOCIAL SECURITY: LESS NOW OR MORE LATER

An economist is someone who knows the price
of everything and the value of nothing .

When the Andersons, Browns, and Caldwells approach retirement they will all face one question: Begin Social Security benefits at age 62 at a reduced rate of 25% or postpone payments until age 66, soon to be 67, for full benefits? Which course results in a greater retirement account?

From an actuarial standpoint the Social Security Administration advises potential retirees that the starting age makes no difference. Actuarial tables are statistical summaries. There are a number of retirees who will live longer than expected; others will live shorter lives. In a sense, then, choice depends on the luck of the draw, general health, and family history.

Financially, the answer depends on three variables. First, each family must have enough funds available to pay for four years of expenses if they postpone Social Security benefits. The second factor is the inflation rate assumed in the retirement model. The third factor, return on investment, is the key variable.

If all three families succeed in generating the necessary retirement funds, or work, they will all be able to finance four years of retirement without Social Security; but which option will result in a greater bank balance at the end of the day? Here is how the break-even ages stack up. The break-even age is defined as the age where the two accounts, one for benefits beginning at age 62 and the other at age 66, become equal. Beyond this age the account with delayed benefits becomes greater.

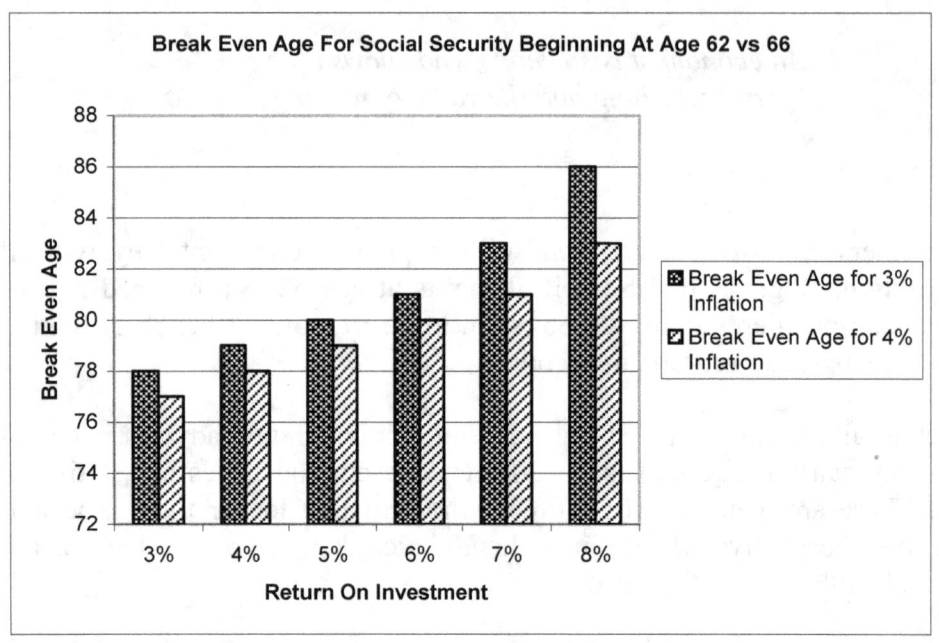

Figure 32
Break Even Ages For Social Security

Assuming the planned 3% rate of inflation and an expected surviving spouse to age 90, the Andersons, who earn 3% on their investments, will break even at age 78. The Andersons postpone Social Security benefits to age 66. The Browns earn 5% on their investments and with a break-even age of 80 they too postpone benefits. The Caldwells earn 8% and their break-even age is 86; they choose to begin Social Security early with a penalty of 25%.

All break even ages occur before the planned 90 year age of the longest survivor, but for the Caldwells the potential enjoyment of four years of slightly greater benefits does not justify the risk of not surviving that long and enjoying less of their potential benefits. The Caldwells' decision will prove even better if they succeed in earning a return on investment greater than 8%, a reasonable assumption.

CHAPTER 13: WEAVING A SAFETY NET

If you want a guarantee, buy a toaster!

Statistical averages can lead to a sense of false security. The long-term return since 1950 on investment from the S&P500, for example, is greater than 10% per year, but this does not mean that the index acts like a bank account returning 10% compound interest year after year. The valuation of the stock market fluctuates. Sometimes the market's precipitous drop makes headline news; other times its rapid increase is viewed as euphoric, with no real substance.

The nightmare scenario for a retiree fully invested in the S&P500 is for the market to drop suddenly the day retirement begins. Withdrawals would then come from a shrinking financial base that would be difficult to rebuild.

This situation is not unrealistic. Consider the history of the S&P500 from 1950 in the next three graphs:

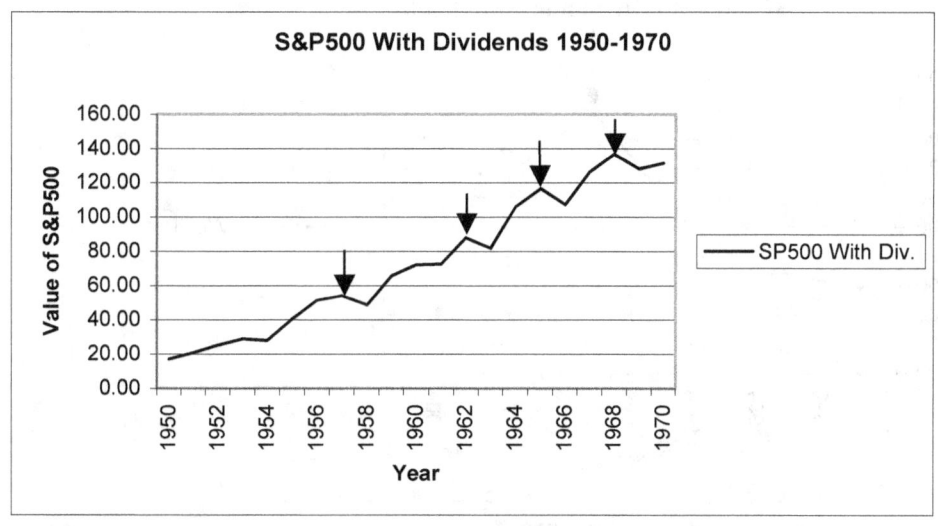

Figure 33
S&P500 Historical Values 1950 To 1970

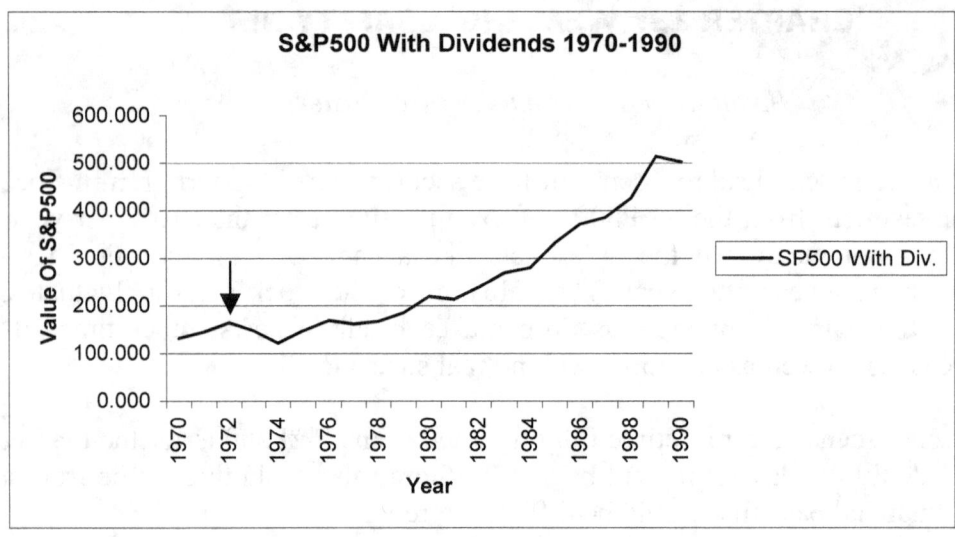

Figure 34
S&P500 Historical Values 1970 To 1990

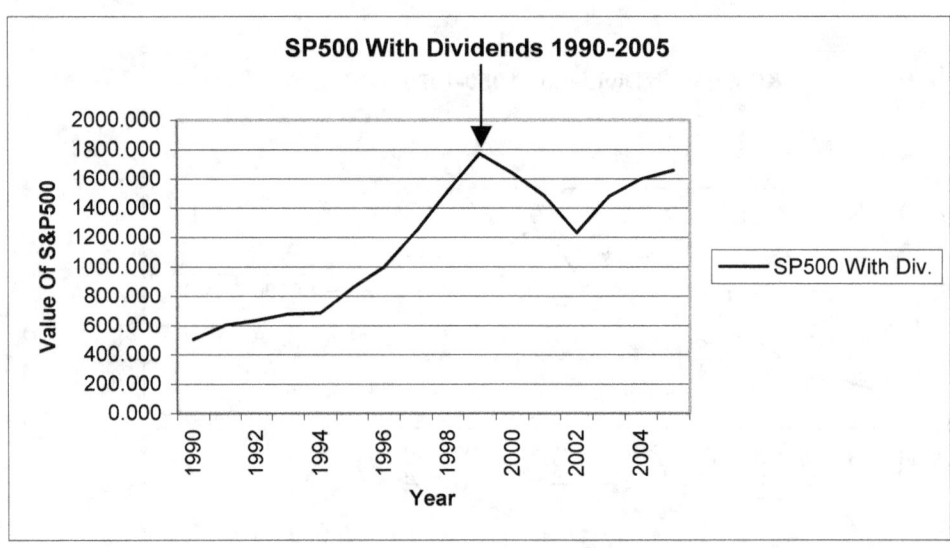

Figure 35
S&P500 Historical Values 1990 To 2005

Anyone retiring in the years marked with an arrow would experience a marked drop in the value of the retirement account just as funds would begin to be drawn out. The bear market of 2000, for example, lasted three years and took more than six years to return to its original value. Retirement plans fully invested in the stock market may have experienced irreparable damage as funds were drawn from increasingly smaller accounts. The depression of 1929 was a catastrophe that took more than 20 years to repair.

Meet The Eflands

Like their counterparts, the Eflands also live in Median, USA, and earn the median household income of $46,326. Their approach to retirement planning is similar to the Caldwell's. They contribute 4% of their gross income to the company's savings plan and the company matches their contribution for a total savings rate of 8% per year.

Like the Caldwells, they invest their savings in an S&P500 index fund, expecting an average return on investment of at least 8%. They are 30 years old and plan to retire at age 65. They realize that the stock market can fluctuate widely. Accordingly, they want to combine the returns of the S&P500 with a safety net. The goal is to guarantee a cash flow equal to the amount they will need to meet expenses in their retirement years even if their timing does not turn out to be optimal.

First, they need to determine the cash flow needed from their retirement account.

Retirement Budget Sources

Age	Social Security	Retirement Account	Total Budget
65	$ 59,963	$ 45,624	$ 105,587
66	$ 61,762	$ 46,993	$ 108,755
67	$ 63,615	$ 48,403	$ 112,018
68	$ 65,524	$ 49,855	$ 115,379
69	$ 67,489	$ 51,350	$ 118,849
70	$ 69,514	$ 52,891	$ 122,405
71	$ 71,599	$ 54,478	$ 126,077
72	$ 73,747	$ 56,112	$ 129,859
73	$ 75,960	$ 57,795	$ 133,755
74	$ 78,239	$ 59,529	$ 137,768
75	$ 80,586	$ 61,315	$ 141,901
76	$ 83,003	$ 63,155	$ 146,158
77	$ 85,493	$ 65,049	$ 150,542
78	$ 88,058	$ 67,001	$ 155,059
79	$ 90,700	$ 69,011	$ 159,711
80	$ 93,421	$ 71,081	$ 164,502
81	$ 96,223	$ 73,214	$ 169,437
82	$ 99,110	$ 75,410	$ 174,520
83	$ 102,083	$ 77,672	$ 179,755
84	$ 105,146	$ 80,002	$ 185,148
85	$ 108,300	$ 82,402	$ 190,702
86	$ 111,549	$ 84,875	$ 196,424
87	$ 114,896	$ 87,421	$ 202,317
88	$ 118,343	$ 90,043	$ 208,386
89	$ 121,893	$ 92,745	$ 214,638
90	0	0	0

Figure 36
Efland Budget Sources

The table above identifies the full retirement budget, based on 3% inflation, and the source of each cash flow. The Social Security estimates are based on figures provided by the Social Security Administration.

When the Eflands are 65 years old, for example, they will need to withdraw $45,624 from their personal retirement account. When they are 89 years old they will need to withdraw $92,745 to meet living expenses to age 90, their target end age.

Annuities offer an attractive package in that they can guarantee income until the death of both spouses. In some circumstances an annuity can be a useful component of an overall retirement plan. A longevity annuity merits special attention and is discussed in the next chapter.

The Efland's goal is to guarantee that the necessary cash will be available regardless of stock market behavior during their retirement years. They also realize that this insurance will require additional contributions into their retirement fund throughout their working years. They want to know how much more they need to set aside to achieve this objective.

The Eflands reject equity-indexed annuities because of low return on investment. Similarly they reject bonds because they simply do not have the cash necessary to purchase enough bonds to support them throughout their retirement.

They decide on a strategy that combines investing in the stock market during their working years with a companion strategy of building a portfolio of laddered U.S. treasury TIPS, Treasury Inflation Protected Securities. By delaying the purchase of this lower yield investment until age 64, the Eflands hope to have enough assets to purchase a guaranteed income to age 90. TIPS will protect the Eflands from inflation, guaranteeing an inflation-adjusted spending level. Historically, TIPS have returned a yield to maturity of 2.5% net of inflation.

Here is how they work. A $1,000, 2.5% yield to maturity TIPS due in 20 years, for example, would sell for about $1,000. Every six months the principal is adjusted to account for the change in the Consumer Price Index and interest is paid on the adjusted principal. In 20 years, when the bond matures, each bond will redeem the full $1,000 plus the accumulated inflation adjustments. If inflation during the 20 years were a constant 3%, for example, the adjusted face value of the bond would be about $1,806. TIPS offer an ideal vehicle for locking in a guaranteed return net of inflation. Implicit in this approach is that the Eflands will reinvest the interest payments at an inflation-adjusted return of at least 2.5%

This is just what the Eflands need. They find that by increasing their yearly contribution to their retirement fund by $727, less than 2% of their gross income, they can meet their objective. This discovery is quite startling because with this mixed mode approach they can guarantee principal, investment return, and cash flow at a very modest cost. The plan combines the best features of annuities and the security of U.S. treasuries into one affordable package. They decide to contribute an extra 1% to the company savings plan and let the company match their contribution with another 1%. Most brokerage firms sell TIPS at no charge because they make a profit from the difference between their buy and sell prices. The US Treasury also sells TIPS directly to consumers through their on-line auction. In essence, then, this investment has no expense to the investor. The Eflands now need a strategy where they use some of their retirement funds invested in the S&P500 to purchase a number of TIPS that will mature one after the other in a laddered maturity sequence. This sequence will match the withdrawals from their retirement fund. Here is what they develop.

Age	TIPS Purchase Plan
64	$ 831,000

In order to moderate the amount of additional contributions they must make to their retirement fund, the Eflands decide to decrease slightly their standard of living for age 65 and beyond. Instead of the predicted $45,264 from their retirement fund (Figure 36--column 2, line1), they arbitrarily reduce this figure by 3% to $44,295. At age 64, before they retire, they purchase 25 laddered TIPS bundles from their S&P500 account at a cost of $831,000. Here is a snapshot of their purchase plan:

TIPS SAFETY NET

	TIPS Yield	2.50%		Inflation	3.00%	Inflation Adjusted Value Of TIPS At Maturity
Age At Purchase	Number Of TIPS	Cost of TIPS	Years to Maturity	Age at Maturity	Inflation Adjusted Retirement Contribution	
64	44	$44,000	1	65	$ 44,295	$ 45,100
64	43	$43,000	2	66	$ 44,295	$ 45,177
64	42	$42,000	3	67	$ 44,295	$ 45,229
64	41	$41,000	4	68	$ 44,295	$ 45,256
64	40	$40,000	5	69	$ 44,295	$ 45,256
64	39	$39,000	6	70	$ 44,295	$ 45,228
64	38	$38,000	7	71	$ 44,295	$ 45,170
64	37	$37,000	8	72	$ 44,295	$ 45,081
64	36	$36,000	9	73	$ 44,295	$ 44,959
64	35	$35,000	10	74	$ 44,295	$ 44,803
64	34	$34,000	11	75	$ 44,295	$ 44,611
64	33	$33,000	12	76	$ 44,295	$ 44,381
64	33	$33,000	13	77	$ 44,295	$ 45,491
64	32	$32,000	14	78	$ 44,295	$ 45,215
64	31	$31,000	15	79	$ 44,295	$ 44,897
64	30	$30,000	16	80	$ 44,295	$ 44,535
64	30	$30,000	17	81	$ 44,295	$ 45,649
64	29	$29,000	18	82	$ 44,295	$ 45,230
64	28	$28,000	19	83	$ 44,295	$ 44,762
64	28	$28,000	20	84	$ 44,295	$ 45,881
64	27	$27,000	21	85	$ 44,295	$ 45,349
64	26	$26,000	22	86	$ 44,295	$ 44,761
64	26	$26,000	23	87	$ 44,295	$ 45,880
64	25	$25,000	24	88	$ 44,295	$ 45,218
64	24	$24,000	25	89	$ 44,295	$ 44,495
	Total Cost	$831,000				

Figure 37
Efland TIPS Purchase Plan

TIPS are purchased in units of $1,000 face value, so the Eflands first need to determine how many units they need for any one year. Since TIPS are inflation protected, all the Eflands need to do is purchase enough units to yield the retirement account contribution to the spending budget. $44,295 is the inflation-adjusted contribution from the retirement fund for the rest of their lives. To finance their retirement at age 65, for example they discount $44,295 by one year at 2.5%, divide by 1000 and round up to the next whole number. Discounting means dividing $44,295 by one plus the interest rate, 1.025. For age 65, they purchase 44 TIPS. For age 66, they discount $44,295 at 2.5% for two years and purchase 43 TIPS. They repeat this process 25 times, spending a total of $831,000. As the TIPS mature each year, the Eflands will be able to spend an inflation adjusted amount equal to $44,295 plus the inflation adjusted contribution from Social Security. Figure 38 is a snapshot of the Efland's retirement account from age 30 to 65. In order to meet their financial retirement objective the Eflands must now determine the required first year contribution to their retirement plan. To do this, they take $832,825 (Figure 38--$831,000+$1,825, their nest egg at age 64) and divide this number from a factor from Table 4. The factor they need is at the intersection of 34, the number of years to when they plan to purchase the TIPS, and 8%, their expected return on investment. Dividing $832,825 by 219.165, they compute $3,800 as the first year contribution to their retirement fund, an increase of $727 over the Caldwells. They will need to inflate this yearly contribution by the inflation factor.

Efland Risk Of Ruin

The Efland's inflation-adjusted return on investment is 2.5%, standard deviation is 0% because TIPS held to maturity do not change in value, and MRL is 22. Their required retirement nest egg at age 65 will be $832,825 (Figure 38--$831,000+$1,825); their inflation-adjusted withdrawal will be $44,295. The spending rate, S, will be 5.3%. Their probability of running out of funds while still alive is about:

$$\textbf{Risk of Ruin}(\text{Efland}) = 25\%$$

Ironically, in their quest to secure a stable retirement income, the Eflands have actually increased their probability of depleting their funds while still alive. In estimating the number of laddered TIPS they need, the Eflands assumed that neither of them would live beyond the age of 90. As it turns out, there is a non-zero probability that one of them will live beyond the age of 90 and that there will be no funds left to draw from.

Placing the entire retirement nest egg in a fixed income portfolio that is drawn down yearly to meet living expenses runs a high risk of ruin.

Age	S&P500 Account	
30	$0	
31	$3,800	<1ST Year
32	$8,018	
33	$12,691	
34	$17,858	
35	$23,564	
36	$29,854	
37	$36,780	
38	$44,396	
39	$52,762	
40	$61,941	
41	$72,003	
42	$83,023	
43	$95,083	
44	$108,270	
45	$122,679	
46	$138,414	
47	$155,585	
48	$174,313	
49	$194,727	
50	$216,968	
51	$241,189	
52	$267,553	
53	$296,239	
54	$327,437	
55	$361,357	
56	$398,222	
57	$438,275	
58	$481,778	
59	$529,014	
60	$580,290	
61	$635,937	
62	$696,312	Purchase
63	$761,802	TIPS
64	$1,825	<< $831,000

Age	S&P500 Account
65	$12,353
66	$13,341
67	$14,408
68	$15,561
69	$16,806
70	$18,150
71	$19,602
72	$21,170
73	$22,864
74	$24,693
75	$26,668
76	$28,802
77	$31,106
78	$33,594
79	$36,282
80	$39,185
81	$42,319
82	$45,705
83	$112,462
84	$121,458
85	$131,175
86	$141,669
87	$153,003
88	$165,243
89	$178,462
90	$192,739

Figure 38
Efland Retirement Funds

CHAPTER 14: GUARANTEED INCOME FOR LIFE

An economist is someone who gets rich
explaining to others why they are poor.

When the Eflands planned their purchase of TIPS they estimated that at least one of them would live to age 90. Their neighbors, the Finegolds, have a history of longevity in their families but when they tried to weave a retirement income safety net, they discovered that they simply did not have the capital to purchase enough TIPS to cover expenses to age 100. Similarly, the required saving rate they would have to meet during their working years to achieve this additional goal was more than they could afford.

The Finegolds decide to solve this problem with a two-pronged approach. Like the Eflands, they finance their retirement from age 65 to 85 by purchasing TIPS. They finance the remainder of their lives from age 85 onwards with the purchase of a longevity annuity.

The longevity annuity is simply income insurance that promises to pay a set amount to the owner for the rest of his or her life beginning at a certain age. Like a zero coupon bond, the annuity sells at a discount because no payment is made for a number of years. A zero coupon bond pays no interest during its lifetime but pays its face value at maturity. A 2.5%, zero coupon bond due in 25 years, for example, would sell for only about $540 and yield $1,000 at maturity. The annuity cost is further discounted by the mortality factor. A 65-year old male, for example, has a 50% probability of being alive at age 85. So, a longevity annuity can be purchased for about half the cost of an equivalent zero coupon bond; but, unlike a bond, the longevity annuity pays only if the owner is alive. This type of annuity has no cash value and cannot be inherited. It is purely income insurance.

The cost of longevity insurance depends on: the age of the owner, the sex of the owner, prevailing interest rates, and the number of years to commencement of payments. With interest rates of 5%, age 65, and commencement of payments at age 85, Mr. Finegold's annuity will cost about $1 for every $1 paid per year starting at age 85. Mrs. Finegold's annuity will cost $1.38 for the same coverage. A joint annuity will cost $1.82. Because the joint annuity is more expensive, the Finegolds decide to purchase separate annuities.

Here is a snapshot of the Finegold's purchase plan:

TIPS SAFETY NET AND LONGEVITY ANNUITY

TIPS Yield	2.50%			Inflation	3.00%		
Age At Purchase	Number Of TIPS	Cost of TIPS	Years to Maturity	Age at Maturity	Inflation Adjusted Retirement Contribution		Inflation Adjusted Value Of TIPS At Maturity
64	44	$44,000	1	65	$ 44,295		$ 45,100
64	43	$43,000	2	66	$ 44,295		$ 45,177
64	42	$42,000	3	67	$ 44,295		$ 45,229
64	41	$41,000	4	68	$ 44,295		$ 45,256
64	40	$40,000	5	69	$ 44,295		$ 45,256
64	39	$39,000	6	70	$ 44,295		$ 45,228
64	38	$38,000	7	71	$ 44,295		$ 45,170
64	37	$37,000	8	72	$ 44,295		$ 45,081
64	36	$36,000	9	73	$ 44,295		$ 44,959
64	35	$35,000	10	74	$ 44,295		$ 44,803
64	34	$34,000	11	75	$ 44,295		$ 44,611
64	33	$33,000	12	76	$ 44,295		$ 44,381
64	33	$33,000	13	77	$ 44,295		$ 45,491
64	32	$32,000	14	78	$ 44,295		$ 45,215
64	31	$31,000	15	79	$ 44,295		$ 44,897
64	30	$30,000	16	80	$ 44,295		$ 44,535
64	30	$30,000	17	81	$ 44,295		$ 45,649
64	29	$29,000	18	82	$ 44,295		$ 45,230
64	28	$28,000	19	83	$ 44,295		$ 44,762
64	28	$28,000	20	84	$ 44,295		$ 45,881
64	27	$27,000	21	85	$ 44,295		$ 45,349
64	26	$26,000	22	86	$ 44,295		$ 44,761
64	26	$26,000	23	87	$ 44,295		$ 45,880
64	25	$25,000	24	88	$ 44,295		$ 45,218
64	24	$24,000	25	89	$ 44,295		$ 44,495
	Total Cost	$831,000					**Annuity Payments**
65		$120,000	<< Annuity Purchase				$ 100,000 per year

Figure 39
Finegold TIPS Purchase Plan And Longevity Annuity

The Finegold's TIPS purchase plan matches the Eflands. At 65, however, the Finegolds purchase a longevity annuity for $120,000, $50,000 for Mr. Finegold and \$50,720 for Mrs. Finegold. Their income is now guaranteed from age 85 onward.

Age	S&P500 Account	
30	$0	
31	$4,300	<1ST Year
32	$9,073	
33	$14,361	
34	$20,208	
35	$26,665	
36	$33,783	
37	$41,620	
38	$50,238	
39	$59,704	
40	$70,091	
41	$81,477	
42	$93,947	
43	$107,594	
44	$122,516	
45	$138,821	
46	$156,626	
47	$176,057	
48	$197,248	
49	$220,349	
50	$245,517	
51	$272,924	
52	$302,758	
53	$335,217	
54	$370,521	
55	$408,904	
56	$450,620	
57	$495,942	
58	$545,169	
59	$598,621	
60	$656,644	
61	$719,613	
62	$787,932	Purchase
63	$862,039	TIPS
64	$111,408	<< $831,000

Age	S&P500 Account	<< Longevity Annuity Cost $ 120,000
65	$12,067	
66	$13,033	
67	$14,075	
68	$15,201	
69	$16,418	
70	$17,731	
71	$19,150	
72	$20,681	
73	$22,336	
74	$24,123	
75	$26,053	
76	$28,137	
77	$30,388	
78	$32,819	
79	$35,444	
80	$38,280	
81	$41,342	
82	$44,650	
83	$48,222	
84	$52,079	
85	$56,246	
86	$60,745	
87	$65,605	
88	$70,854	
89	$76,522	
90	$82,644	

Figure 40
Finegold Retirement Account

With living expenses covered by TIPS from age 65 to 85 and the longevity insurance commencing payments at age 85, the Finegolds are set for the rest of their lives. The Finegolds finance the cost of this additional insurance by making a higher contribution to their retirement plans. They contribute $4,300 at age 30 compared to the Efland's $4,000. They compute this amount dividing $942,408, their required total nest egg at age 64, by the Table 4 factor, 219.165.

In setting the contributions from the longevity annuities at what appears to be a comfortable $100,000 per year starting at age 85 and beyond, the Finegolds still run the risk of underestimating the inflation rate. When one of them passes away, also, the surviving member will lose the partner's contribution from the longevity annuity. Longevity annuities can be purchased with riders to cover inflation and survivor benefits but each additional feature increases the cost of the coverage. The cost-benefit-risk ratio is a problem that each family must resolve in their most comfortable way. TIPS, although more costly, provide inflation protection.

Finegold Risk Of Ruin

With TIPS covering inflation-adjusted living expenses from age 65 to 85 and longevity annuities covering inflation-adjusted living expenses for each of them for the rest of their lives, the risk of ruin is:

$$\text{Risk of Ruin(Finegold)} = 0\%$$

Formulas can give a false sense of security. As with any annuity, the promise of future payments is only as good as the financial integrity of the insurance company. The longevity annuity, however, carries an additional risk. Almost all forms of annuities consist of two phases—the accumulation phase and the payout phase. During the accumulation phase the investor can request the return of all funds, usually by paying a penalty. Not so with the longevity annuity. Once purchased, there is no recourse and if the insurance company was to default on its future obligations, the retiree's state of residence may provide only a limited safety net.

Anyone contemplating a longevity annuity, or any annuity for that matter, should research thoroughly the future financial health of the company. Ultimately, risk of future default remains a distinct possibility that can be reduced to zero only with the purchase of government securities such as TIPS. The allocation of 10% to 20% of assets to an annuity, can, however, be part of an overall retirement plan.

CHAPTER 15: YOUR RETIREMENT BUDGET PLANNER

Retirement
Budget Planner

	Base Information			
1	Budget In Today's Dollars			$
2	Years To Retirement			
3	Longest Years Of Retirement			
4	Age			
5	Enter Inflation Factor (3% or 4%)			
6	Desired Fraction Of Total Budget (80% to 100% recommended)			
7	Target Return On Investments			
8	Future Value Factor From Table 1 (Intersection of years to ret. and inflation %)			
9	Future Tot. Ret. Budget Factor (Table 4 or 7 int. of yrs to ret. and inflation%)			
10	First Payment Factor (Table 2 or 5 intersection of years to ret. and years of ret.)			
11	Multiplication Factor (Table 3 or 6 intersection of years to ret. and inv. return %)			
12	Table 8 (3% infl.) Table 9 (4% infl.) int. of years of retirement and inv. return %			
13	Line 11 x Line 12 + 0.01			
14	Future Value Factor For Existing Funds (Table 1 int. of yrs to ret & inv. return%)			
15	Total Percent Contribution To Company Retirement Plan			
16	Budget In Future Dollars (Line 1 x Line 8)	$		
	Initial Computation Of Required Yearly Contributions			
17	Future Budget Factor (Line 10 x Line 13 x Line 16)	$		
18	Total Future Value Of Budget (Line 9 x Line 17)		$	
	Compute Impact Of All Present Savings And Retirement Plans			
19	Present Value Of All Tax Deferred Accounts	$		
20	Future Value Of All Tax Deferred Accounts (Line 14 x Line 19)		$	
21	Total Yearly Contributions to Retirement Plan (Line 1 x Line15)	$		
22	Future Value Of Retirement Plans (Line 9 x Line 21)		$	
23	Savings	$		
24	Future Value Of Savings (Line 14 x Line 23)		$	
25	Total Future Values From Retirement Plan and Savings (L 20 + 22 + L 24)		$	
26	Fractional Reduction (Line 25/Line 18)		%	
	Compute Impact Of Future Social Security Payments			
27	Yearly Social Security Payment In Future Dollars from Social Security statement		$	
28	Fractional Reduction (Line 27/Line 16)		%	
29	1.0 – Line 6		%	
30	Sum (L 26 + L 28 + L 29)		%	
31	1.0 – Line 30			%
32	Budget to finance (Line 1 x Line 31)			$
	Compute Yearly Payment To Meet Retirement Budget			
33	**Yearly Payment** (Line 10 x Line 13 x Line 32)			$

In order to determine the amount of the first year payment you need to fill out your Retirement Budget Planner. Each line of the planner is explained in detail here. The Caldewll planner illustrates an example. First you need to determine your estimated rate of inflation; you have two choices, 3% or 4%. Your choice for inflation determines which tables in Appendix 1 you will use.

Line 1
Enter the total present budget, including income taxes
Line 2
Enter years to retirement
Line 3
Enter years of longest retirement
Line 4
Enter Your Age
Line 5
Enter Rate Of Inflation (3% or 4%)
Line 6
Enter Desired Percent Of Total Budget For Retirement (80%-100% recommended)
Line 7
Enter Targeted Return On Investment in percent
Line 8
Future Value Factor, Table 1; use the 3% or 4% (depending on assumed inflation factor) column at the intersection with the number of years to retirement.
Line 9
Future Tot. Ret. Budget Factor (Table 4 for 3% inflation or Table 7 for 4% inflation) use value at the intersection of the return on investment column with the row of number of years to retirement.
Line 10
First Payment Factor (Table 2 for 3% inflation or Table 5 for 4% inflation) enter value at intersection year of retirement column with years to retirement row.
Line 11
Multiplication Factor (Table 3 or 6 for 3% or 4% inflation; enter value at intersection of return on investment in % and years TO retirement.)
Line 12
(Table 8 or 9 for 3% or 4% inflation) enter value at intersection of return on investment in % and years OF retirement.
Line 13
Line 11 times Line 12 plus 0.01

Line 14
Future Value Factor For Existing Funds (Table 1 enter value at intersection of return on investment with number of years to retirement.)
Line 15
Percent Of Income Paid Yearly Into Company Retirement Plan

Factor in impact of present savings, if any
Line 16
Budget In Future Dollars (Line 1 x Line 8)
Line 17
Future Budget Factor (L 10 x L 13 x L 16)
Line 18
Total Future Value Of Budget (Line 9 x Line 17)
Line 19
Present Value Of Tax Deferred Accounts
Line 20
Future Value Of Tax Deferred Accounts (Line 14 x Line 19)
Line 21
Total Yearly Contributions To Retirement Plan (Line 1 x Line 15)
Line 22
Future Value Of Retirement Plan (Line 9 x Line 21)
Line 23
Enter Amount Of Personal Savings
Line 24
Future Value Of Savings (Line 14 x Line 23)
Line 25
Total Future Value Of All Funds (Sum L 20, L 22, L 24)
Line 26
Percent Reduction (Line 25 divided by Line 18)
Line 27
Yearly Social Security Payments In Future Dollars (Check with the Social Security Administration)
Line 28
Fractional Reduction (Line 27 divided by Line 16)
Line 29
1.0 minus Line 6
Line 30
Add Line 26, 28 and Line 29
Line 31
1.0 minus Line 30

Line 32
Budget To Finance (Line 1 x Line 31)
Line 33
Yearly Payment To Retirement Fund (L 10 x L 13 x L 32)

This is the first payment you must make into your retirement fund. If you increase your payments by your assumed inflation rate of 3% or 4% each year, and invest all your funds at your estimated rate of investment return, you will meet all the requirements to fund your stated years of retirement. The table parameters are designed to yield a well-padded retirement budget that errs on the side of caution reducing the risk of financial ruin probability to about 10%. The parameters result in larger financial padding when fewer years are left to accumulate wealth.

Readers are invited to visit the free interactive web-based spreadsheet:

http://mysite.verizon.net/geode/loafer.xls

for a plug-and-play version of the retirement budget sheet where they can try various scenarios. The spreadsheet incorporates all the tables and formulas to compute entries for the retirement budget planner and the risk of ruin.

APPENDIX 1

Tables

TABLE 1

Years To Retirement	<<<Inflation Rate Or Return On Investment>>>							
	3%	4%	5%	6%	7%	8%	9%	10%
1	1.0300	1.0400	1.0500	1.0600	1.0700	1.0800	1.0900	1.1000
2	1.0609	1.0816	1.1025	1.1236	1.1449	1.1664	1.1881	1.2100
3	1.0927	1.1249	1.1576	1.1910	1.2250	1.2597	1.2950	1.3310
4	1.1255	1.1699	1.2155	1.2625	1.3108	1.3605	1.4116	1.4641
5	1.1593	1.2167	1.2763	1.3382	1.4026	1.4693	1.5386	1.6105
6	1.1941	1.2653	1.3401	1.4185	1.5007	1.5869	1.6771	1.7716
7	1.2299	1.3159	1.4071	1.5036	1.6058	1.7138	1.8280	1.9487
8	1.2668	1.3686	1.4775	1.5938	1.7182	1.8509	1.9926	2.1436
9	1.3048	1.4233	1.5513	1.6895	1.8385	1.9990	2.1719	2.3579
10	1.3439	1.4802	1.6289	1.7908	1.9672	2.1589	2.3674	2.5937
11	1.3842	1.5395	1.7103	1.8983	2.1049	2.3316	2.5804	2.8531
12	1.4258	1.6010	1.7959	2.0122	2.2522	2.5182	2.8127	3.1384
13	1.4685	1.6651	1.8856	2.1329	2.4098	2.7196	3.0658	3.4523
14	1.5126	1.7317	1.9799	2.2609	2.5785	2.9372	3.3417	3.7975
15	1.5580	1.8009	2.0789	2.3966	2.7590	3.1722	3.6425	4.1772
16	1.6047	1.8730	2.1829	2.5404	2.9522	3.4259	3.9703	4.5950
17	1.6528	1.9479	2.2920	2.6928	3.1588	3.7000	4.3276	5.0545
18	1.7024	2.0258	2.4066	2.8543	3.3799	3.9960	4.7171	5.5599
19	1.7535	2.1068	2.5270	3.0256	3.6165	4.3157	5.1417	6.1159
20	1.8061	2.1911	2.6533	3.2071	3.8697	4.6610	5.6044	6.7275
21	1.8603	2.2788	2.7860	3.3996	4.1406	5.0338	6.1088	7.4002
22	1.9161	2.3699	2.9253	3.6035	4.4304	5.4365	6.6586	8.1403
23	1.9736	2.4647	3.0715	3.8197	4.7405	5.8715	7.2579	8.9543
24	2.0328	2.5633	3.2251	4.0489	5.0724	6.3412	7.9111	9.8497
25	2.0938	2.6658	3.3864	4.2919	5.4274	6.8485	8.6231	10.8347
26	2.1566	2.7725	3.5557	4.5494	5.8074	7.3964	9.3992	11.9182
27	2.2213	2.8834	3.7335	4.8223	6.2139	7.9881	10.2451	13.1100
28	2.2879	2.9987	3.9201	5.1117	6.6488	8.6271	11.1671	14.4210
29	2.3566	3.1187	4.1161	5.4184	7.1143	9.3173	12.1722	15.8631
30	2.4273	3.2434	4.3219	5.7435	7.6123	10.0627	13.2677	17.4494
31	2.5001	3.3731	4.5380	6.0881	8.1451	10.8677	14.4618	19.1943
32	2.5751	3.5081	4.7649	6.4534	8.7153	11.7371	15.7633	21.1138
33	2.6523	3.6484	5.0032	6.8406	9.3253	12.6760	17.1820	23.2252
34	2.7319	3.7943	5.2533	7.2510	9.9781	13.6901	18.7284	25.5477
35	2.8139	3.9461	5.5160	7.6861	10.6766	14.7853	20.4140	28.1024
36	2.8983	4.1039	5.7918	8.1473	11.4239	15.9682	22.2512	30.9127
37	2.9852	4.2681	6.0814	8.6361	12.2236	17.2456	24.2538	34.0039
38	3.0748	4.4388	6.3855	9.1543	13.0793	18.6253	26.4367	37.4043
39	3.1670	4.6164	6.7048	9.7035	13.9948	20.1153	28.8160	41.1448
40	3.2620	4.8010	7.0400	10.2857	14.9745	21.7245	31.4094	45.2593
41	3.3599	4.9931	7.3920	10.9029	16.0227	23.4625	34.2363	49.7852
42	3.4607	5.1928	7.7616	11.5570	17.1443	25.3395	37.3175	54.7637

TABLE 2

Years To Retirement	1st Year Payment Per Dollar Factors For 3% Inflation <<<Years Of Retirement>>>								
	1	5	10	15	20	25	30	35	40
1	1.0300	5.1500	10.3000	15.4500	20.6000	25.7500	30.9000	36.0500	41.2000
2	0.5150	2.5750	5.1500	7.7250	10.3000	12.8750	15.4500	18.0250	20.6000
3	0.3433	1.7167	3.4333	5.1500	6.8667	8.5833	10.3000	12.0167	13.7333
4	0.2575	1.2875	2.5750	3.8625	5.1500	6.4375	7.7250	9.0125	10.3000
5	0.2060	1.0300	2.0600	3.0900	4.1200	5.1500	6.1800	7.2100	8.2400
6	0.1717	0.8583	1.7167	2.5750	3.4333	4.2917	5.1500	6.0083	6.8667
7	0.1471	0.7357	1.4714	2.2071	2.9429	3.6786	4.4143	5.1500	5.8857
8	0.1288	0.6438	1.2875	1.9313	2.5750	3.2188	3.8625	4.5063	5.1500
9	0.1144	0.5722	1.1444	1.7167	2.2889	2.8611	3.4333	4.0056	4.5778
10	0.1030	0.5150	1.0300	1.5450	2.0600	2.5750	3.0900	3.6050	4.1200
11	0.0936	0.4682	0.9364	1.4045	1.8727	2.3409	2.8091	3.2773	3.7455
12	0.0858	0.4292	0.8583	1.2875	1.7167	2.1458	2.5750	3.0042	3.4333
13	0.0792	0.3962	0.7923	1.1885	1.5846	1.9808	2.3769	2.7731	3.1692
14	0.0736	0.3679	0.7357	1.1036	1.4714	1.8393	2.2071	2.5750	2.9429
15	0.0687	0.3433	0.6867	1.0300	1.3733	1.7167	2.0600	2.4033	2.7467
16	0.0644	0.3219	0.6438	0.9656	1.2875	1.6094	1.9313	2.2531	2.5750
17	0.0606	0.3029	0.6059	0.9088	1.2118	1.5147	1.8176	2.1206	2.4235
18	0.0572	0.2861	0.5722	0.8583	1.1444	1.4306	1.7167	2.0028	2.2889
19	0.0542	0.2711	0.5421	0.8132	1.0842	1.3553	1.6263	1.8974	2.1684
20	0.0515	0.2575	0.5150	0.7725	1.0300	1.2875	1.5450	1.8025	2.0600
21	0.0490	0.2452	0.4905	0.7357	0.9810	1.2262	1.4714	1.7167	1.9619
22	0.0468	0.2341	0.4682	0.7023	0.9364	1.1705	1.4045	1.6386	1.8727
23	0.0448	0.2239	0.4478	0.6717	0.8957	1.1196	1.3435	1.5674	1.7913
24	0.0429	0.2146	0.4292	0.6438	0.8583	1.0729	1.2875	1.5021	1.7167
25	0.0412	0.2060	0.4120	0.6180	0.8240	1.0300	1.2360	1.4420	1.6480
26	0.0396	0.1981	0.3962	0.5942	0.7923	0.9904	1.1885	1.3865	1.5846
27	0.0381	0.1907	0.3815	0.5722	0.7630	0.9537	1.1444	1.3352	1.5259
28	0.0368	0.1839	0.3679	0.5518	0.7357	0.9196	1.1036	1.2875	1.4714
29	0.0355	0.1776	0.3552	0.5328	0.7103	0.8879	1.0655	1.2431	1.4207
30	0.0343	0.1717	0.3433	0.5150	0.6867	0.8583	1.0300	1.2017	1.3733
31	0.0332	0.1661	0.3323	0.4984	0.6645	0.8306	0.9968	1.1629	1.3290
32	0.0322	0.1609	0.3219	0.4828	0.6438	0.8047	0.9656	1.1266	1.2875
33	0.0312	0.1561	0.3121	0.4682	0.6242	0.7803	0.9364	1.0924	1.2485
34	0.0303	0.1515	0.3029	0.4544	0.6059	0.7574	0.9088	1.0603	1.2118
35	0.0294	0.1471	0.2943	0.4414	0.5886	0.7357	0.8829	1.0300	1.1771
36	0.0286	0.1431	0.2861	0.4292	0.5722	0.7153	0.8583	1.0014	1.1444
37	0.0278	0.1392	0.2784	0.4176	0.5568	0.6959	0.8351	0.9743	1.1135
38	0.0271	0.1355	0.2711	0.4066	0.5421	0.6776	0.8132	0.9487	1.0842
39	0.0264	0.1321	0.2641	0.3962	0.5282	0.6603	0.7923	0.9244	1.0564
40	0.0258	0.1288	0.2575	0.3863	0.5150	0.6438	0.7725	0.9013	1.0300
41	0.0251	0.1256	0.2512	0.3768	0.5024	0.6280	0.7537	0.8793	1.0049
42	0.0245	0.1226	0.2452	0.3679	0.4905	0.6131	0.7357	0.8583	0.9810

Table 3
Inflation And Return Adjustment Factor--3%

Years To Retirement	<<< Return On Investment >>>						
	3%	4%	5%	6%	7%	8%	9%
1	1	1	1	1	1	1	1
2	1	0.9952	0.9904	0.9856	0.9810	0.9763	0.9717
3	1	0.9904	0.9808	0.9714	0.9622	0.9530	0.9439
4	1	0.9856	0.9713	0.9574	0.9436	0.9301	0.9167
5	1	0.9808	0.9619	0.9434	0.9253	0.9075	0.8901
6	1	0.9760	0.9525	0.9296	0.9072	0.8853	0.8640
7	1	0.9712	0.9432	0.9160	0.8894	0.8636	0.8384
8	1	0.9665	0.9340	0.9024	0.8718	0.8421	0.8134
9	1	0.9618	0.9248	0.8891	0.8545	0.8211	0.7889
10	1	0.9571	0.9157	0.8758	0.8374	0.8005	0.7649
11	1	0.9524	0.9066	0.8627	0.8206	0.7802	0.7415
12	1	0.9477	0.8976	0.8498	0.8040	0.7603	0.7186
13	1	0.9431	0.8887	0.8369	0.7876	0.7407	0.6962
14	1	0.9384	0.8798	0.8242	0.7715	0.7216	0.6744
15	1	0.9338	0.8710	0.8117	0.7556	0.7028	0.6531
16	1	0.9292	0.8623	0.7993	0.7400	0.6844	0.6322
17	1	0.9246	0.8536	0.7870	0.7246	0.6663	0.6119
18	1	0.9200	0.8450	0.7748	0.7094	0.6486	0.5921
19	1	0.9154	0.8364	0.7628	0.6945	0.6312	0.5728
20	1	0.9109	0.8279	0.7510	0.6798	0.6142	0.5540
21	1	0.9063	0.8195	0.7392	0.6653	0.5976	0.5356
22	1	0.9018	0.8111	0.7276	0.6511	0.5813	0.5178
23	1	0.8973	0.8028	0.7161	0.6371	0.5653	0.5004
24	1	0.8928	0.7945	0.7048	0.6233	0.5497	0.4835
25	1	0.8884	0.7863	0.6936	0.6098	0.5344	0.4670
26	1	0.8839	0.7782	0.6825	0.5965	0.5195	0.4510
27	1	0.8795	0.7701	0.6716	0.5834	0.5049	0.4354
28	1	0.8750	0.7621	0.6608	0.5705	0.4906	0.4203
29	1	0.8706	0.7542	0.6501	0.5578	0.4766	0.4056
30	1	0.8662	0.7463	0.6396	0.5454	0.4630	0.3913
31	1	0.8619	0.7384	0.6291	0.5332	0.4496	0.3774
32	1	0.8575	0.7307	0.6188	0.5212	0.4366	0.3640
33	1	0.8532	0.7230	0.6087	0.5094	0.4239	0.3509
34	1	0.8488	0.7153	0.5987	0.4978	0.4115	0.3382
35	1	0.8445	0.7077	0.5887	0.4864	0.3994	0.3260
36	1	0.8402	0.7002	0.5790	0.4753	0.3875	0.3141
37	1	0.8359	0.6927	0.5693	0.4643	0.3760	0.3025
38	1	0.8316	0.6853	0.5598	0.4536	0.3647	0.2913
39	1	0.8274	0.6779	0.5504	0.4430	0.3538	0.2805
40	1	0.8231	0.6706	0.5411	0.4326	0.3431	0.2700
41	1	0.8189	0.6634	0.5319	0.4225	0.3327	0.2599
42	1	0.8147	0.6562	0.5229	0.4125	0.3225	0.2501

TABLE 4

Years To Retirement	Value of Retirement Fund Accumulating at $1/Yr Increased at 3% Inflation And Earning Listed Return On Investment							
	3%	4%	5%	6%	7%	8%	9%	<<Return On Investment
1	1	1	1	1	1	1	1	
2	2.060	2.070	2.080	2.090	2.100	2.110	2.120	
3	3.183	3.214	3.245	3.276	3.308	3.340	3.372	
4	4.371	4.435	4.500	4.566	4.632	4.700	4.768	
5	5.628	5.738	5.850	5.965	6.082	6.201	6.322	
6	6.956	7.127	7.302	7.482	7.667	7.856	8.051	
7	8.358	8.606	8.861	9.125	9.398	9.679	9.969	
8	9.839	10.180	10.534	10.903	11.285	11.683	12.097	
9	11.401	11.854	12.328	12.824	13.342	13.885	14.452	
10	13.048	13.633	14.249	14.898	15.581	16.300	17.057	
11	14.783	15.522	16.305	17.135	18.015	18.948	19.937	
12	16.611	17.527	18.505	19.548	20.661	21.848	23.115	
13	18.535	19.654	20.856	22.146	23.533	25.022	26.621	
14	20.559	21.909	23.367	24.944	26.649	28.492	30.486	
15	22.689	24.298	26.048	27.953	30.027	32.284	34.742	
16	24.927	26.827	28.908	31.188	33.686	36.425	39.427	
17	27.280	29.505	31.959	34.664	37.649	40.943	44.580	
18	29.751	32.338	35.209	38.397	41.937	45.872	50.245	
19	32.346	35.334	38.672	42.403	46.576	51.244	56.469	
20	35.070	38.501	42.359	46.701	51.589	57.097	63.305	
21	37.928	41.847	46.283	51.309	57.007	63.471	70.809	
22	40.926	45.382	50.458	56.248	62.857	70.409	79.042	
23	44.070	49.113	54.897	61.539	69.174	77.958	88.071	
24	47.366	53.051	59.615	67.205	75.989	86.168	97.971	
25	50.820	57.206	64.629	73.270	83.341	95.094	108.822	
26	54.438	61.588	69.954	79.760	91.269	104.795	120.709	
27	58.228	66.208	75.608	86.702	99.814	115.335	133.730	
28	62.196	71.078	81.610	94.125	109.023	126.784	147.987	
29	66.350	76.209	87.979	102.061	118.942	139.214	163.594	
30	70.697	81.614	94.734	110.541	129.625	152.708	180.674	
31	75.245	87.305	101.898	119.601	141.126	167.352	199.361	
32	80.003	93.298	109.493	129.277	153.505	183.240	219.804	
33	84.978	99.605	117.543	139.608	166.825	200.474	242.162	
34	90.179	106.241	126.072	150.637	181.155	219.165	266.608	
35	95.617	113.223	135.108	162.407	196.568	239.430	293.335	
36	101.299	120.565	144.677	174.966	213.142	261.398	322.549	
37	107.236	128.286	154.809	188.362	230.960	285.208	354.477	
38	113.439	136.403	165.535	202.649	250.112	311.010	389.365	
39	119.917	144.934	176.886	217.883	270.695	338.965	427.483	
40	126.681	153.898	188.898	234.123	292.811	369.250	469.123	
41	133.744	163.316	201.604	251.432	316.569	402.052	514.606	
42	141.116	173.209	215.045	269.878	342.089	437.576	564.281	

TABLE 5

Years To Retirement	1st Year Payment Per Dollar Factor Based on 4% Inflation								
	<<<Years Of Retirement>>>								
	1	5	10	15	20	25	30	35	40
1	1.04	5.2	10.4	15.6	20.8	26	31.2	36.4	41.6
2	0.5200	2.6000	5.2000	7.8000	10.4000	13.0000	15.6000	18.2000	20.8000
3	0.3467	1.7333	3.4667	5.2000	6.9333	8.6667	10.4000	12.1333	13.8667
4	0.2600	1.3000	2.6000	3.9000	5.2000	6.5000	7.8000	9.1000	10.4000
5	0.2080	1.0400	2.0800	3.1200	4.1600	5.2000	6.2400	7.2800	8.3200
6	0.1733	0.8667	1.7333	2.6000	3.4667	4.3333	5.2000	6.0667	6.9333
7	0.1486	0.7429	1.4857	2.2286	2.9714	3.7143	4.4571	5.2000	5.9429
8	0.1300	0.6500	1.3000	1.9500	2.6000	3.2500	3.9000	4.5500	5.2000
9	0.1156	0.5778	1.1556	1.7333	2.3111	2.8889	3.4667	4.0444	4.6222
10	0.1040	0.5200	1.0400	1.5600	2.0800	2.6000	3.1200	3.6400	4.1600
11	0.0945	0.4727	0.9455	1.4182	1.8909	2.3636	2.8364	3.3091	3.7818
12	0.0867	0.4333	0.8667	1.3000	1.7333	2.1667	2.6000	3.0333	3.4667
13	0.0800	0.4000	0.8000	1.2000	1.6000	2.0000	2.4000	2.8000	3.2000
14	0.0743	0.3714	0.7429	1.1143	1.4857	1.8571	2.2286	2.6000	2.9714
15	0.0693	0.3467	0.6933	1.0400	1.3867	1.7333	2.0800	2.4267	2.7733
16	0.0650	0.3250	0.6500	0.9750	1.3000	1.6250	1.9500	2.2750	2.6000
17	0.0612	0.3059	0.6118	0.9176	1.2235	1.5294	1.8353	2.1412	2.4471
18	0.0578	0.2889	0.5778	0.8667	1.1556	1.4444	1.7333	2.0222	2.3111
19	0.0547	0.2737	0.5474	0.8211	1.0947	1.3684	1.6421	1.9158	2.1895
20	0.0520	0.2600	0.5200	0.7800	1.0400	1.3000	1.5600	1.8200	2.0800
21	0.0495	0.2476	0.4952	0.7429	0.9905	1.2381	1.4857	1.7333	1.9810
22	0.0473	0.2364	0.4727	0.7091	0.9455	1.1818	1.4182	1.6545	1.8909
23	0.0452	0.2261	0.4522	0.6783	0.9043	1.1304	1.3565	1.5826	1.8087
24	0.0433	0.2167	0.4333	0.6500	0.8667	1.0833	1.3000	1.5167	1.7333
25	0.0416	0.2080	0.4160	0.6240	0.8320	1.0400	1.2480	1.4560	1.6640
26	0.0400	0.2000	0.4000	0.6000	0.8000	1.0000	1.2000	1.4000	1.6000
27	0.0385	0.1926	0.3852	0.5778	0.7704	0.9630	1.1556	1.3481	1.5407
28	0.0371	0.1857	0.3714	0.5571	0.7429	0.9286	1.1143	1.3000	1.4857
29	0.0359	0.1793	0.3586	0.5379	0.7172	0.8966	1.0759	1.2552	1.4345
30	0.0347	0.1733	0.3467	0.5200	0.6933	0.8667	1.0400	1.2133	1.3867
31	0.0335	0.1677	0.3355	0.5032	0.6710	0.8387	1.0065	1.1742	1.3419
32	0.0325	0.1625	0.3250	0.4875	0.6500	0.8125	0.9750	1.1375	1.3000
33	0.0315	0.1576	0.3152	0.4727	0.6303	0.7879	0.9455	1.1030	1.2606
34	0.0306	0.1529	0.3059	0.4588	0.6118	0.7647	0.9176	1.0706	1.2235
35	0.0297	0.1486	0.2971	0.4457	0.5943	0.7429	0.8914	1.0400	1.1886
36	0.0289	0.1444	0.2889	0.4333	0.5778	0.7222	0.8667	1.0111	1.1556
37	0.0281	0.1405	0.2811	0.4216	0.5622	0.7027	0.8432	0.9838	1.1243
38	0.0274	0.1368	0.2737	0.4105	0.5474	0.6842	0.8211	0.9579	1.0947
39	0.0267	0.1333	0.2667	0.4000	0.5333	0.6667	0.8000	0.9333	1.0667
40	0.0260	0.1300	0.2600	0.3900	0.5200	0.6500	0.7800	0.9100	1.0400
41	0.0254	0.1268	0.2537	0.3805	0.5073	0.6341	0.7610	0.8878	1.0146
42	0.0248	0.1238	0.2476	0.3714	0.4952	0.6190	0.7429	0.8667	0.9905

Table 6
Inflation And Return Adjustment Factor--4%

Years to Retirement	<<< Return On Investment >>>					
	4%	5%	6%	7%	8%	9%
1	1	1	1	1	1	1
2	1	0.9952	0.9905	0.9858	0.9811	0.9765
3	1	0.9904	0.9810	0.9717	0.9625	0.9534
4	1	0.9857	0.9716	0.9578	0.9441	0.9307
5	1	0.9810	0.9623	0.9439	0.9260	0.9084
6	1	0.9762	0.9530	0.9303	0.9081	0.8864
7	1	0.9715	0.9438	0.9167	0.8904	0.8648
8	1	0.9668	0.9346	0.9033	0.8730	0.8436
9	1	0.9622	0.9255	0.8901	0.8558	0.8227
10	1	0.9575	0.9165	0.8770	0.8389	0.8022
11	1	0.9528	0.9075	0.8640	0.8222	0.7821
12	1	0.9482	0.8986	0.8511	0.8057	0.7623
13	1	0.9436	0.8897	0.8384	0.7895	0.7429
14	1	0.9390	0.8809	0.8258	0.7735	0.7239
15	1	0.9344	0.8722	0.8133	0.7577	0.7053
16	1	0.9298	0.8635	0.8010	0.7422	0.6869
17	1	0.9253	0.8549	0.7888	0.7269	0.6690
18	1	0.9207	0.8464	0.7768	0.7118	0.6514
19	1	0.9162	0.8379	0.7649	0.6970	0.6341
20	1	0.9117	0.8295	0.7531	0.6824	0.6172
21	1	0.9072	0.8211	0.7414	0.6681	0.6007
22	1	0.9027	0.8128	0.7299	0.6539	0.5845
23	1	0.8983	0.8045	0.7185	0.6400	0.5686
24	1	0.8938	0.7963	0.7073	0.6263	0.5531
25	1	0.8894	0.7882	0.6961	0.6128	0.5379
26	1	0.8850	0.7801	0.6852	0.5996	0.5230
27	1	0.8806	0.7721	0.6743	0.5866	0.5084
28	1	0.8762	0.7642	0.6635	0.5738	0.4942
29	1	0.8718	0.7563	0.6529	0.5612	0.4803
30	1	0.8675	0.7484	0.6425	0.5488	0.4667
31	1	0.8631	0.7407	0.6321	0.5366	0.4534
32	1	0.8588	0.7330	0.6219	0.5247	0.4404
33	1	0.8545	0.7253	0.6118	0.5129	0.4277
34	1	0.8502	0.7177	0.6018	0.5014	0.4153
35	1	0.8459	0.7102	0.5919	0.4901	0.4032
36	1	0.8416	0.7027	0.5822	0.4789	0.3914
37	1	0.8374	0.6953	0.5726	0.4680	0.3799
38	1	0.8332	0.6879	0.5631	0.4573	0.3686
39	1	0.8289	0.6806	0.5538	0.4468	0.3577
40	1	0.8247	0.6733	0.5445	0.4364	0.3470
41	1	0.8205	0.6662	0.5354	0.4263	0.3366
42	1	0.8164	0.6590	0.5264	0.4164	0.3264

TABLE 7

Years To Retirement	Value of Retirement Fund Accumulating at $1/Yr Increased at 4% Inflation And Earning Listed Return On Investment							
	4%	5%	6%	7%	8%	9%	10%	<<Return On Investment
1	1.0000	1.0000	1.0000	1.0000	1.0000	1.0000	1.0000	
2	2.0800	2.0900	2.1000	2.1100	2.1200	2.1300	2.1400	
3	3.2448	3.2761	3.3076	3.3393	3.3712	3.4033	3.4356	
4	4.4995	4.5648	4.6309	4.6979	4.7658	4.8345	4.9040	
5	5.8493	5.9629	6.0786	6.1966	6.3169	6.4394	6.5643	
6	7.2999	7.4777	7.6600	7.8470	8.0389	8.2356	8.4374	
7	8.8572	9.1169	9.3849	9.6617	9.9473	10.2421	10.5464	
8	10.5275	10.8886	11.2640	11.6539	12.0590	12.4799	12.9170	
9	12.3171	12.8016	13.3084	13.8382	14.3923	14.9716	15.5773	
10	14.2331	14.8650	15.5302	16.2302	16.9670	17.7424	18.5583	
11	16.2827	17.0885	17.9422	18.8466	19.8046	20.8194	21.8944	
12	18.4734	19.4824	20.5582	21.7053	22.9284	24.2327	25.6233	
13	20.8134	22.0576	23.3927	24.8257	26.3638	28.0146	29.7866	
14	23.3110	24.8255	26.4614	28.2286	30.1379	32.2010	34.4304	
15	25.9751	27.7985	29.7807	31.9363	34.2806	36.8308	39.6051	
16	28.8151	30.9893	33.3685	35.9728	38.8240	41.9465	45.3665	
17	31.8407	34.4118	37.2436	40.3638	43.8029	47.5947	51.7762	
18	35.0622	38.0803	41.4261	45.1372	49.2551	53.8261	58.9017	
19	38.4905	42.0101	45.9375	50.3226	55.2213	60.6962	66.8177	
20	42.1370	46.2175	50.8006	55.9520	61.7459	68.2658	75.6063	
21	46.0136	50.7195	56.0398	62.0598	68.8766	76.6008	85.3580	
22	50.1329	55.5342	61.6809	68.6828	76.6655	85.7736	96.1726	
23	54.5081	60.6808	67.7517	75.8605	85.1687	95.8632	108.1598	
24	59.1532	66.1796	74.2815	83.6354	94.4469	106.9556	121.4405	
25	64.0826	72.0519	81.3017	92.0532	104.5660	119.1449	136.1478	
26	69.3117	78.3203	88.8457	101.1628	115.5971	132.5338	152.4284	
27	74.8567	85.0088	96.9489	111.0166	127.6173	147.2343	170.4438	
28	80.7343	92.1426	105.6492	121.6712	140.7101	163.3687	190.3715	
29	86.9624	99.7484	114.9868	133.1869	154.9656	181.0706	212.4074	
30	93.5595	107.8545	125.0047	145.6286	170.4815	200.4856	236.7667	
31	100.5453	116.4906	135.7484	159.0660	187.3634	221.7727	263.6868	
32	107.9403	125.6883	147.2664	173.5737	205.7256	245.1054	293.4286	
33	115.7659	135.4807	159.6104	189.2320	225.6917	270.6729	326.2796	
34	124.0450	145.9032	172.8354	206.1266	247.3954	298.6819	362.5559	
35	132.8011	156.9926	186.9999	224.3497	270.9814	329.3576	402.6058	
36	142.0592	168.7884	202.1660	244.0003	296.6060	362.9458	446.8125	
37	151.8455	181.3317	218.3999	265.1843	324.4384	399.7149	495.5976	
38	162.1874	194.6664	235.7719	288.0153	354.6616	439.9573	549.4255	
39	173.1137	208.8385	254.3571	312.6151	387.4733	483.9923	608.8069	
40	184.6546	223.8968	274.2349	339.1146	423.0875	532.1680	674.3039	
41	196.8418	239.8927	295.4900	367.6536	461.7355	584.8641	746.5353	
42	209.7086	256.8804	318.2124	398.3824	503.6674	642.4950	826.1819	

	Table 8--3% Inflation						
	<<<Return On Investment>>>						
Years Of Retirement	3%	4%	5%	6%	7%	8%	9%
10	1.00	0.96	0.93	0.90	0.87	0.85	0.82
15	1.00	0.94	0.89	0.84	0.80	0.76	0.72
20	1.00	0.92	0.85	0.79	0.73	0.68	0.64
25	1.00	0.90	0.81	0.74	0.68	0.62	0.58
30	1.00	0.88	0.78	0.69	0.62	0.57	0.52
35	1.00	0.86	0.74	0.65	0.58	0.52	0.47
40	1.00	0.84	0.71	0.61	0.54	0.47	0.42

	Table 9--4%Inflation						
	<<<Return On Investment>>>						
Years Of Retirement	3%	4%	5%	6%	7%	8%	9%
10	1.00	0.96	0.92	0.89	0.85	0.82	0.79
15	1.00	0.94	0.88	0.83	0.78	0.74	0.70
20	1.00	0.92	0.84	0.78	0.72	0.67	0.62
25	1.00	0.90	0.81	0.73	0.67	0.61	0.56
30	1.00	0.88	0.77	0.69	0.60	0.55	0.50
35	1.00	0.86	0.74	0.65	0.57	0.51	0.46
40	1.00	0.84	0.71	0.61	0.53	0.47	0.40

APPENDIX 2

Investment Recommendations

*An economist is someone who doesn't know what he
is talking about and makes you feel it's your fault.*

Mutual Funds

Vanguard 500 Index Fund. Vanguard Telephone: (877) 662-7747.
www.vanguard.com. Vanguard is the leader for investments in the S&P500 with
the lowest expense ratio in the industry.

Exchange Traded Funds

Ticker symbol: SPY. S&P500, purchased from a brokerage house. This fund
emulates the S&P500 and each component is weighted according to the
capitalization of the company. The largest 30-50 companies determine to a large
extent the performance of the S&P500 index.

Ticker symbol: RSP. Rydex Equal Weight S&P500, purchased from a brokerage
house. Each component of the S&P500 in this fund carries equal weight; thus, this
fund is influenced less by the performance of companies with large capitalization
giving equal influence to all components of the index.

Longevity Annuity

The Hartford Life Insurance Company. MET Life Insurance Company.

SLOW COOKING

A banker walks into a pizzeria and orders a pizza. When the pizza is cooked, he goes up to the counter to get it. There, a clerk asks him: "Should I cut it into six pieces or eight pieces?" The banker replies: "I'm feeling rather hungry. You'd better cut it into eight pieces."

Now that your money is working for you instead of the other way around, you have time to pursue some of the pleasures of life—like eating and drinking. As in financial planning, good things take time. Foods that are cooked slowly at low temperature are moist and full of flavor. The long cooking time also allows smoke to permeate the food, adding yet another delicious dimension to food consumption.

The secret to preparing succulent meat is brining. Although counter-intuitive, like the stock market, soaking meat in salt water actually increases the water content of the meat; and improves its moisture. Other chemical changes also take place in the meat; but trust me, all you need to know is that it works like magic, especially with pork and fowl.

The Wet Brine

1	cup water
¾	Tbsp kosher salt, such as Morton's

Prepare enough brine to cover meat; self-sealing plastic bags work great. Rinse and dry after brining.

Food	Brining Time (refrigerated)
Turkey	12-24 hours
Chicken	6-12 hours
Chicken pieces	2 hours
Pork tenderloin	2 hours
Pork shoulder	12-24 hours
Boston butt	4-6 hours
Tuna steaks, any thick fish	1 hour
Shrimp, shell on	45 minutes

The Dry Brine

2 parts kosher salt
1 part dark brown sugar, lightly packed

This brine is the first step in making smoked salmon.

The Dry Rub

5	Tbsp chili powder
4	Tbsp ground cumin
2	Tbsp ground coriander
1	Tbsp Kosher salt
1	Tbsp Cajun seasoning
1 ½	Tbsp dark brown sugar
1	tsp black pepper
2	Tbsp paprika
1	Tbsp garlic powder
1	Tbsp onion powder
1	tsp ground allspice
½	tsp ground cloves

This dry rub is great for pork dishes. Make a lot of it and keep in a jar; no refrigeration required.

The Wet Rub

1	14-oz bottle of ketchup
½	cup water
1	tsp liquid smoke
4	Tbsp Worcestershire sauce
3	tsp mustard
6	Tbsp butter
¼	tsp red pepper
1	tsp ground cumin
1	tsp garlic powder
1	tsp onion powder
1	Tbsp paprika
2	Tbsp cider vinegar
1	Tbsp hot sauce

Mix all ingredients and bring to a simmer for 15 minutes. Keep refrigerated.

The Fish Sauce

1	cup mayonnaise
1/3	cup grated horseradish or horseradish sauce
1	Tbsp lemon juice
1	tsp Dijon style mustard

Mix all ingredients together. Keep refrigerated.

The Smoker

Luhr Jensen makes the best smoker on the market; it is called the Luhr Jensen Little Chief smoker. This is an electric smoker that comes in different sizes. The correct temperature is pre-set, so no worrying about this setting. The smoker is available from on-line suppliers and costs about $100. A recipe booklet comes with the smoker as a bonus.

RECIPES

*Economists are people who are too smart for their
own good and not smart enough for anyone else's.*

Slow Roasted Boston Butt

Boston butt is an inexpensive cut of meat and it is very fatty. The fat keeps the meat moist during cooking so wet brining is not necessary. Rub the meat with a tablespoon of kosher salt then rub generously with the dry rub. Place in the smoker for three hours.

A clay pot is the ideal cooking utensil; but, failing that, any oven proof Dutch oven will do. Place the roast in the pot, cover tightly, turn the temperature to 200 degrees F, and cook for 11 hours. Enjoy the aroma!

When done, remove the meat from the pot. Pour the juices in a degreasing cup. Place the degreased juices in a small pan, bring to a slow boil and simmer until half the volume remains. Add cider vinegar to taste.

In the meantime, shred the meat, removing all the remaining fat and any skin. Add salt and pepper to taste and then add some of the vinegar-meat-juice saving the rest as additional sauce. Adjust seasonings to taste.

Serve with baked sweet potato fries and lots of cold beer.

Pork Ribs

Buy a full set of ribs. Avoid baby back ribs because they don't have enough fat. Rub generously with the dry rub on both sides. Smoke for one and a half hours.

I prefer a gas grill because I can control the temperature better. In any case, set a grill temperature of 230 to 250 degrees F. Place the ribs on the grill, close the lid, and grill for 2 hours. Turn the ribs over and grill another 2 hours. Finally, turn the ribs meat side up and slather generously with the wet rub. Fifteen minutes later, repeat the slathering. Cook another 15 to 30 minutes or until the rub has glazed over and the meat is shrinking from the bones. Let rest 15 minutes and then cut into individual ribs with a butcher knife. Serve with hush puppies and lots of cold beer.

Porchetta

Porchetta is an Italian specialty found near Rome and also in Umbria. It is a fully de-boned pig, stuffed with herbs and then slow roasted to a beautiful golden brown finish with a crispy skin.

For home use buy a picnic shoulder or fresh ham; be sure that there is plenty of skin. Have the butcher de-bone the roast, or you can do it yourself. Brine the meat in the wet brine overnight. Rinse and dry. Process finely plenty of fresh rosemary, sage, and half a pod of garlic. Add six slices of chopped bacon. Add salt and pepper to taste.

Cut various slits inside the meat, leaving the skin intact. Rub the herb mixture in the slits and all over the inside of the roast. Close the roast and tie with twine.

Set the grill at a temperature of 500 degrees F. Place the roast on the grill and lower temperature to 280 degrees F. Cook roast for two hours. Turn roast over and cook another two hours or until the internal temperature of the meat is 205 degrees F. The skin should be a beautiful golden brown and crispy.

Allow roast to rest a half hour. Slice and serve with lots of cold beer and good artisan bread.

Smoked Salmon

This recipe will not only save you a lot of money, it will also make more friends for you than ever before. Buy two skinned full salmon fillets; warehouse stores such as Costco and Sam's stock this item regularly.

Completely cover both sides of each fillet with the dry brine. Refrigerate for two hours. Rinse the fish and allow drying for an hour on a rack. Start the smoker. I use hickory chips because they are readily available and impart a strong smoke flavor.

Cut each fillet into three pieces. Place the thinner end pieces of the fish on the top rack because they will need to be removed first. Place all the portions on the remaining racks.

Smoking times depend on the outdoor temperature; experience is the best teacher. In general, smoke for two to three hours, replacing the wood chips as needed; and then check the top pieces. If they are starting to turn a darker brown on the edges and feel firm, remove them from the smoker and place them on a rack to cool. After one or two additional hours (again replacing wood chips as necessary), check the rest of the fillets. They should have a beautiful brown sheen, may ooze a little oil and they should feel fairly firm to the touch. If so, they are ready. Remove the fillets from the smoker and place them on a rack. Allow the fillets to cool and then seal each piece with plastic wrap and refrigerate overnight.

Invite your investment buddies over, buy a couple of bottles of champagne or Italian Prosecco, buy a carton of whipped cream cheese, buy a box of unflavored Melba toast, bring out the sliced salmon. If you can hold the hordes back, here is how the fish should be served. Spread a small amount of whipped cream cheese on a Melba toast; place a slice of the smoked fish on the cheese and then top with a dab of the fish sauce. Eat slowly, if you can.

Barbequed Shrimp

Buy a pound of fresh shrimp with the head on (if possible). Fresh shrimp work best because they have the best texture; frozen shrimp are a poor second.

Brine the shrimp in the wet brine for one hour; if you wish, you may add a teaspoon of Zatarin's liquid crab and shrimp boil to the brine. In the meantime, melt a half stick of salt butter and add it to a half-cup of vegetable oil. Add four to six tablespoons of the dry rub. Add the brined shrimp to this mixture and refrigerate for one hour.

Remove shrimp from refrigerator and drain sauce into a small pan. Simmer for 10 minutes and pour into a bowl. Add some melted butter if you wish.

Light a grill to maximum temperature. Place the shrimp on long skewers and when the temperature has reached 500 degrees F, place the shrimp on the grill, closing the lid. Cook for exactly two minutes for large shrimp. Turn shrimp over and cook another two minutes. Remove from heat and serve immediately, dipping the shrimp in the sauce. The shrimp shells will be so crunchy and flavorful that some people eat head and all. Serve with French bread and lots of cold beer.

Smoked Turkey

Prepare enough wet brine to cover a whole turkey. To the brine add a sliced sweet onion, a peeled head of garlic, two chopped celery stalks and two peeled and chopped carrots. Place the turkey in a large plastic bag, add the brine, twist the bag to remove all the air and refrigerate for 12 to 24 hours.

Remove the turkey from the brine and rinse inside and out. In the meantime, fire up the smoker with hickory chips. Smoke the turkey for three hours.

Remove the turkey from the smoker and allow it to rest for 45 minutes on a plastic bag filled with ice, breast-side down. Finish cooking the turkey in an oven, grill, or rotisserie. Baste every 15 minutes with melted butter and a little soy sauce.

In the meantime, rinse the vegetables that were in the brine and sauté them in oil and butter on medium heat until nicely caramelized (browned). Reserve for later.

Remove the turkey when it reaches a temperature of 165 degrees F near the thigh and allow it to rest for 20 minutes. Carve the turkey, sprinkle with kosher salt, freshly ground pepper, freshly chopped sage, freshly chopped thyme, and the reserved, sautéed vegetables. Top with the meat juices from the roasting pan. Serve with a slightly cooled pinot noir. You will want to celebrate Thanksgiving more than once a year!

Smoked Scallops With Smoky Mayonnaise

1   lb. fresh scallops
1   cup dry brine

1   cup mayonnaise
1   tsp Dijon mustard
2   tsp lemon juice

Purchase the largest and freshest scallops available. Cover the scallops with the dry brine for 30 minutes. In the meantime fire up the smoker with hickory chips.

Rinse the scallops in running water, dry, and smoke them for one hour. Place the scallops in a microwave-proof dish and cook them at 80% microwave power until just done, an internal temperature of 145 degrees F.

Remove the scallops from the dish and allow them to cool in the refrigerator. The scallops will have oozed juices in the baking dish; the juices will have a divine aroma of hickory smoke. Mix the mayonnaise, mustard, lemon juice and a couple of tablespoons of the juices together. Adjust seasonings to taste. Refrigerate overnight.

The next day slice the scallops across the grain into thick wafer-like slices. Serve with the smoky mayonnaise. Serve with champagne, Riesling or beer. Watch out for the marauding hordes!

Smoked Pork Tenderloin

2	pork tenderloins
2	cups wet brine
	the zest of two large oranges
½	cup chopped fresh sage
¼	cup chopped fresh rosemary
½	cup olive oil
2	Tbsp apple jelly
1	tsp kosher salt
½	tsp freshly ground black pepper

Brine pork for two hours in the wet brine.

In the meantime, mix rest of ingredients together into a thick paste.

Fire up the smoker with hickory chips. Remove the meat from the brine, rinse well, and pat dry. Smoke for one hour. In the meantime fire up the grill to maximum and pre-heat for 15 minutes.

Remove the meat from the smoker and slather with the orange zest paste. Place on the hot grill, close the lid, and cook for seven minutes. Turn over and cook another six minutes. Turn off grill and allow to rest for five minutes or until the internal temperature of the meat reaches 155 degrees F. Remove from grill and allow to rest 15 minutes.

Slice across the grain into thick slices and top with the meat juices that will have collected during the cutting process. Serve with a chilled rosé or Riesling.

Edie's Brisket

4	lbs beef brisket (preferably point cut, otherwise flat cut)
2	cups wet brine
½	cup dry rub
1 1/2	cups wet rub

The point cut has more fat and yields a moister roast. If unavailable, the flat cut will have to do. Brine the brisket for two hours. Rinse and then pat dry. Score the fatty side in a diamond pattern and then pat all over with the dry rub. Smoke for two hours or sprinkle with two tablespoons of liquid smoke.

Wrap the brisket in aluminum foil, place in a baking pan and bake at 325 degrees F for 4 hours or until the internal temperature reaches 205 to 210 degrees F. Remove from heat and allow to rest for 20 minutes. In the meantime, warm the wet rub.

Remove brisket from the foil. Boil down the meat juices rapidly to half the original volume and then add to the warmed, wet rub. In the meantime, slice the brisket thinly across the grain. Slather liberally with the warmed wet rub. Serve with cold beer or a fine zinfandel.

Bricked Chicken

1	whole chicken split in half
2	cups wet brine

2	tsp kosher salt
½	tsp freshly ground pepper
2	Tbsp olive oil

¼   cup chopped, mixed, fresh herbs: sage, rosemary, thyme, and oregano

Brine chicken for two hours. Rinse and pat dry. Smoke chicken for one hour or add wood chips when grilling. Before grilling, rub chicken with salt, pepper, and olive oil.

Fire up the grill to medium heat, about 350 to 400 degrees F. Place chicken, skin side up, on the grill, place a brick or cast iron skillet wrapped in aluminum foil on top of the chicken halves. Close the grill lid. Cook for 15 minutes, watching for flare-ups. Turn chicken over, placing the weights on top again, and grill another fifteen to twenty minutes or until the internal meat temperature reaches 165 degrees F. Watch for flare-ups.

Remove from heat. Sprinkle generously with olive oil and fresh herbs. Add salt and pepper to taste. Serve with cold beer or a fine rosé wine.

GLOSSARY

bi-modal distribution	A distribution of values that has the greatest number of occurrences for two values.
cap	Used in equity-indexed annuities to limit the maximum gain for a given time period.
compound interest	Interest that is paid on interest earned.
CPI	Consumer Price Index, a sophisticated model of consumer shopping behavior.
crediting method	Used in equity-indexed annuities to compute the account value at the end of a time period.
Dow Jones Index	An index consisting of 30 major companies.
equity-indexed annuity	An annuity whose value is tied to a market index such as the S&P500.
ECI	Equivalent Compound Interest. See Equivalent Compound Return.
equivalent compound return, ECR	The compound interest a bank would have to pay in order to match the performance of an investment. Also Equivalent Compound Interest.
exchange traded funds	Mutual funds that trade like stock. They usually have lower operating expenses but broker fees are incurred in buying and selling shares.
Gaussian distribution	A distribution of values that resembles a bell curve.
I-bonds	Government bonds with interest tied to inflation.
inflation	The change in the CPI index.
longevity annuity	Guaranteed income for life beginning at an agreed upon age.
mean	The numerical average.
median	The value in the middle position.
month-to-month	Used in equity-indexed annuities to determine the value of an account.
monthly average	Used in equity-indexed annuities to determine the value of an account.
MRL	Median Remaining Life. Given an age for a male or female, half the population will live the remaining life and half will not.
participation rate	Used in equity-indexed annuities to determine the portion of market gain credited to the investor.
risk of ruin	The probability a retiree will deplete the retirement nest egg while still alive.
rule of 72	72 divided by the compound interest rate equals the number of years for an investment to double in value.
S&P500	A weighted index consisting of 500 large capitalization companies.
simple interest	Interest that does not pay interest on interest earned.
standard deviation	In a Gaussian distribution, 67% of the occurrences occur between the average and two standard deviations.
STRIPS	US Treasuries that have been stripped of the interest. Zero coupon bonds.
TIPS	Treasury Inflation Protected Securities, bonds that have the face value tied to inflation.
year-to-year	Used in equity-indexed annuities to credit an investor's account.

INDEX

www.ingramcontent.com/pod-product-compliance
Lightning Source LLC
Chambersburg PA
CBHW081133170526
45165CB00008B/2651